Harold Kalman

MODERN ARCHITECTURE IN ALBERTA

The Citadel Theatre, Edmonton.

MODERN ARCHITECTURE IN ALBERTA

by Trevor Boddy

Alberta Culture and Multiculturalism
and the Canadian Plains Research Center

1987

Canadian Cataloguing in Publication Data

Boddy, Trevor, 1953-

   Modern architecture in Alberta

   Co-published by Alberta Culture.
   Bibliography: p.
   Includes index.
   ISBN 0-88977-046-8 (bound)

1. Architecture - Alberta. 2. Architecture, Modern - 20th
century - Alberta. I. University of Regina. Canadian Plains
Research Center. II. Alberta. Alberta Culture. III. Title.

NA746.A3B62 1987   720'.97123   C86-098080-4

Designed by NICHOLAS NEWBECK DESIGN Victoria, B.C.
Typeset by LEADING TYPE Victoria, B.C.

Printed in Canada by
D.W. Friesen & Sons Ltd.
Altona, Manitoba

CONTENTS

ILLUSTRATIONS

This book is one of a series published jointly by
Alberta Culture and Multiculturalism and the Canadian
Plains Research Center. Their common objective is to
bring to public notice the diverse aspects of Alberta
history as evidenced in Alberta's historical resources.
Each is a result of scholarly research by a specialist
who has approached the significant historical topic
from the vantage point of the associated historic sites.

PREFACE

This book is the result of research conducted under contract with Alberta Culture. The Historic Sites Service of Alberta Culture administers a province-wide programme of designation and classification of historic sites and buildings few of which are from the post-1925 period covered by this study. The intent of the research project was to establish the trends and highlights of the development of Modern architecture in Alberta, with a view to possible further study or designation of the most historically and architecturally significant buildings. As the vast majority of the province's several million buildings were constructed during this period, the emphasis of this study has been placed on public buildings in Edmonton and Calgary. Changing housing forms and styles merit a separate treatment; only a few of the most innovative examples of houses are cited.

Many of the buildings included in the discussion are of questionable aesthetic value, even accounting for the austere, rectilinear design philosophy of Modern architecture. However, they are useful references for sketching the development of attitudes and practices in architectural design over the past fifty years. On the other hand, many excellent buildings, especially from the past decade, had to be excluded from discussion. Rather than exhaustively map the technical and aesthetic developments of the last ten years in Alberta, I have concentrated on earlier decades when the pattern of Modern architecture in Alberta first coalesced.

The tone of the study treads that narrow and dangerous path between architectural history and criticism. The general progression is from art-historical commentary, utilizing stylistic analysis for the oldest buildings, to a more critical and sociological treatment of more recent architectural developments. The overall structure charts change through the history of ideas in architectural design. This process required substantial critical evaluation of such building types as telephone sub-stations, cinemas and gas stations, to which architectural historians have devoted little attention. For the general reader I have offered a brief, schematic overview of the rise of Modern architecture in Europe and the United States. The vast simplification of complex movements needed for this overview is tempered somewhat by some superb illustrations of the key works of the Modern masters kindly provided by the Audio-Visual Archive of the Museum of Modern Art in New York. All photographs are by the author unless otherwise credited.

This book was made possible by the efforts and resources of many individuals and institutions. Foremost are the past and present staff of Alberta Culture, among whom Ian Clarke, Robert Hunter, Frank Korvemaker, Diana Bodnar, and Mark Rasmussen provided excellent and well-directed comments and suggestions. The late Roger Soderstrom guided the project through its earliest phases. Without the encouragement of Dr. John Lunn, this study would never have come about. Annalies Walker and her staff at the Canadian Architectural Archives, University of Calgary, enabled me to make the most of this emerging research centre for the study of twentieth-century Canadian architecture. I am particularly grateful for the help of three architectural historians who have devoted their own attentions to the buildings of this century: Michael McMordie of the University of Calgary, Alan Gowans of the University of Victoria, and David Gebhard of the University of California, Santa Barbara. Practicing and retired architects, as well as archivists and librarians around the province, provided me with invaluable information and opinion. Special thanks must go to the students and faculty of the University of Calgary's Faculty of Environmental Design, where most of this manuscript was written. Earlier versions of portions of the book have appeared in *TRACE, Architect's Forum, The Canadian Architect,* and *Prairie Forum;* I express my gratitude to the editors of these journals for their support. Janet Harper instructed me in the arcane mysteries of a computer text-editing system, among other things.

Five years passed between the completion of the manuscript and its publication. In those years, I have benefitted from the comments of scholarly referees and the editorial attention of Patricia Myers, Richard Goulet and Carl Betke of Alberta Culture and Multiculturalism, and Brian Mlazgar and Gillian Wadsworth Minifie of the Canadian Plains Research Center, University of Regina. A Postscript, 1986, has been added to temper the boomtime tone of the final chapters, and to comment on recent architectural developments.

My sincere thanks to these and many others who have allowed me to make the first inroads into a large and fascinating topic.

Trevor Boddy

OWLEDGEMENTS

Permission has been granted to quote from the following works: University of California Press ("The Modern as Vision of the Whole" by Stephen Spender in Irving Howe, ed., *The Idea of the Modern in Literature and the Arts*); MIT Press (*Collage City* by Colin Rowe and Fred Koetter); Horizon Press (*The Idea of the Modern in Literature and the Arts* edited by Irving Howe); Theatre Projects Consultants of London (Report to the Calgary Performing Arts Centre Advisory Group); State University of New York Press (*The Early Temples of the Mormons: The Architecture of the Millennial Kingdom of the American West* by Laurel B. Andrew); Royal Architectural Institute of Canada (RAIC *Journal*); Alberta Government Telephones (*The Silent Partner*); Douglas Cardinal (*Of the Spirit: Writings of Douglas Cardinal*).

Le Corbusier's scheme for the reconstruction of the Marais area of Paris, *The Voisin plan for rebuilding Paris*. 1925. Model. Photograph courtesy of The Museum of Modern Art, New York.

INTRODUCTION

In a period of a few short years this century, the substance and direction of architecture changed as it seldom has since man first erected barriers against the sky. The rise of Modern architecture swept away many of the evolving traditions of twenty-five hundred years of architectural design, replacing them with the slick and efficient architectural technology that now fills our cities. The introduction and acceptance of Modern architecture was a complex and multi-levelled phenomenon, in which aesthetic theories, social forces, and new technologies intertwined to change the structure of architectural ideas.

The early years of this century saw the development in Europe of an aesthetic philosophy known as modernism that influenced virtually every art form. The modernists sought symbols, forms, media, and ideas suitable to the mechanized spirit of the new age:

> Early in the century, hope was based on the international inter-arts community of the alliance between the ballet, architecture, furniture design, painting, music and poetry, all of them participating in the movement to revolutionize taste, and at the same time make it an operative acting and criticizing force in modern life.[1]

A common element in modernist thought was the desire to break with history. For the early modern architects, this desire for an historical rupture was so strong as to approach eschatology, a doctrine of the end of history. They sought the millenium of rational, functional architecture on a New Jerusalem of high-rise blocks, expansive grids, and single-use zoning. Modernists wanted a city tamed of the passions and the received values of history:

The new architecture was rationally determinable; the new architecture was historically predestined; the new architecture represented the overcoming of history; the new architecture was responsive to the spirit of the age; the new architecture was socially therapeutic; but perhaps above all—the new architecture meant the end to deception, dissimulation, vanity, subterfuge and imposition.[2]

In architecture the modernists attacked what they saw as redundant and functionally useless historicist decoration. One of the more lurid and influential of the critiques of decoration was written by the Viennese architect Adolf Loos. The earliest commentator to apply Freudian theory to aesthetic concerns, Loos associated applied decoration with infantilism, gangsterism and deviant sexual practices in a widely distributed 1908 essay entitled "Ornament and Crime."[3]

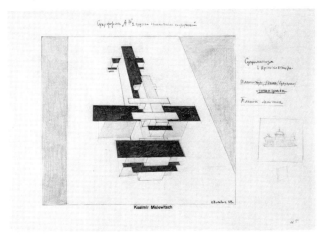

Suprematist Architectural Drawing by Kasimir Malevich, 1924. Pencil, 12 1/4'' x 17 3/8''. Collection, The Museum of Modern Art, New York.

Pablo Picasso's *Guitar*. 1912. Sheet metal and wire, 30 1/2" x 13 1/8" x 7 5/8". Collection, The Museum of Modern Art, New York. Gift of the artist.

Another shared principle of the modernists was the notion that art, like society, should be kept in a constant state of revolutionary change. Tied to this was the idea that meaningful art flows from an artistic avant-garde whose purpose is to lead and shape public opinion. Modernism, in its various and sometimes opposed forms, has dominated virtually every artistic discipline for much of this century. Joyce and Pound in literature, Picasso and Duchamp in the visual arts, Schoenberg and Stravinsky in music—all were caught up in the attempt to make their art more appropriate, more meaningful to a fast-paced and barbarous age. "The past was devoted to answers; the modern period confines itself to questions."[4]

Architecture, more than the other disciplines, was galvanized and changed forever by modernism. An alliance of new aesthetic, social, technological, and intellectual forces swept away such early twentieth-century architectural styles as Expressionism, Art Nouveau, the Picturesque, and variations of Beaux-Arts

classicism in the rise to stylistic dominance of the Modern Movement. While a more "private" art form, such as literature, could tolerate a Bourges, a Hemingway, an Eliot, or a Robbe-Grillet, all working and being read at the same time, architecture underwent a design revolution which both burned its bridges with its past and also effectively obliterated design alternatives to Modern architecture and its variants. The analogy in the field of serious music to what happened in architecture would have been the near-universal acceptance of Arnold Schoenberg's twelve-tone system by classical composers, followed by the near-disappearance of live performances of the works of Bach, Brahms, and Mozart.

Like any revolution, this one in architectural design had its phases and relapses, its Odessa Rebellions and Kerensky Republics. By the early 1930s, the worst of the fighting among architectural theoreticians was over. The new, rational, anti-historical approach stood triumphant and the pioneers of the emerging style, such as Walter Gropius and Le Corbusier, set about building. They encountered a problem inherent in any revolution, the reconciliation of idealistic theory with the pragmatic concerns of architectural practice. In their writing, for example, and in such early projects as Le Corbusier's housing at Pessac or Gropius's units at the Siedlung demonstration project in Stuttgart, the fathers of the Modern Movement in architecture concerned themselves with issues of social change and mass-produced, inexpensive workers' housing. The tenor and tone of the times changed however, and by the 1930s much of the built expression of the ideas of Modern architecture could be seen principally in villas for the rich patrons of the avant-garde.[5]

This book traces Modern architecture's rise to supremacy in the province of Alberta. Beginning with lingering Victorian historicist styles, Alberta was home to various experiments in Art Deco, Art Moderne, and eventually International Style Modern architecture in the period from 1925 to 1950. These experiments, often humble and homely, led to the emergence of mature Modern architecture in the province in the 1950s and 1960s. It is impossible to understand Alberta architecture from this period without noting the international context of theory and practice. Extensive reference is made to architectural developments in Europe and the United States. More than any other art form, and in these years more than any others, internationalism captivated architecture. The progression of design ideas moved almost exclusively from the major world metropoles to developing hinterlands like Alberta. This context of internationalism, of the acceptance and modification of foreign ideas, explains the title selection of *Modern Architecture in Alberta* over *Modern Alberta Architecture* for this book. At its conclusion is an examination of post-1970 alternatives to Modern architecture, and of recent interest in an indigenous, regional design philosophy for Alberta architecture.

The province's rapid growth and urbanization have coincided almost exactly with the reign of Modern architecture, and its square, bare, functional buildings will dominate our cities for the forseeable future. There are few urban centres in the western world which are marked so wholly by Modern architecture as Calgary or Edmonton. This study delineates the history, ideas, and values implicit in Alberta's visual urban environment.

In charting these often nebulous aesthetic and technological changes I have chosen to rely on the somewhat shaky art-historical notion of styles. This method all too often involves stylistic labelling of the most apparent visual elements, without sufficient consideration of the technical and programmatic elements of buildings, invisible to all but the trained eye. Workable definitions of the Art Deco, or the Art Moderne styles in architecture have emerged only recently, and there are the inevitable exceptions and special cases. I have employed the use of stylistic analysis only to give some conceptual order, at times forced, to a complex subject and period.

Le Corbusier, *Still Life*. 1920. Oil on canvas, 31 7/8'' x 39 1/4''. Collection, The Museum of Modern Art, New York. Van Gogh Purchase Fund.

Percy Nobbs's early study for the Arts Building, University of Alberta, circa 1913. The tower was removed from the design before construction. Canadian Architectural Archives, The University of Calgary Library.

THE DECLINE OF HISTORICISM

The Victorian traditions of historicism and eclecticism in architecture were slow to die in Alberta, as elsewhere. While there was much to undermine late nineteenth-century design ideas and approaches, no comprehensive new notion was yet evident to replace them in this part of the world. The 1920s were a period of stylistic and technological uncertainty in Alberta architecture not unlike the 1980s.

Just as the design premises of the Modern Movement in architecture have recently come under attack, during the 1920s the lingering and somewhat debased use of the traditional styles derived from classicism was questioned. The architect of the twenties was likely to question the validity and appropriateness of the classical architectural language of the Doric, Ionic, Corinthian, Tuscan, and Composite orders much as we might question such Modern Movement homilies as "truth in materials" or "less is more." But then, as now, there were no easy alternatives; more substantial reasons were needed for architects to abandon the established, if somewhat over-colloquialized architectural language of the five orders and their humbler equivalents in vernacular building. Late Victorian architecture continued, in increasingly lifeless forms, for want of a new conception of design tailored to the twentieth century.[1]

The reasons for this architectural conservatism include

Workmen at Little's Brick Yard, Victoria Park, Edmonton, circa 1903. E. Brown Collection, Provincial Archives of Alberta.

Stone cutters prepare the foundation of a new building on 100 Avenue, Edmonton. E. Brown Collection, Provincial Archives of Alberta.

the fact that the barely established traditional building crafts in Alberta were greatly damaged by World War I. In the period immediately before the war, Alberta had enjoyed a phenomenal building boom coming on the heels of a land rush and the great flood of new settlers into the west. Calgary, in particular, because of its relative wealth and ties to transcontinental information and immigration flows, had attracted and supported some superb masons, sculptors, carpenters, furniture makers, and other craftsmen. A thriving colony of Scottish stone masons was responsible for the rough hewn, yet elegant sandstone buildings in the city on the Bow that were, and still are, its greatest architectural asset.

World War I and its aftermath were not kind to these craftsmen and their fellows throughout the province. Some locals of artisans' unions reported a 50 percent loss of their members in the trenches of Europe. Those who elected to return to western Canada after the war found mounting tension and dislocation, as evidenced in the Winnipeg General Strike of 1919. Over-construction during the pre-war land boom, tied to serious post-war economic problems, encouraged precious little additional construction in Alberta until well into the 1920s.

A loss of traditional building materials accompanied the loss of traditional building crafts. Pre-war Calgary and district boasted five sandstone quarries. By the late twenties only one remained. Brick factories in Medicine Hat and Edmonton were only just able to hold their own through this bleak period. Lathe-turned wooden columns were rarely found in the houses of the twenties while they had been inexpensive and common a decade earlier. Custom-sculpted elements such as the sandstone Ionic columns from a Medicine Hat house virtually disappeared.

Architecture has had to ride the waves of boom and bust in Alberta. Prairie population growth fluctuated from Canada's fastest before World War I to Canada's slowest during the next thirty years. The very quantities of civic boosterism which had fostered Calgary and Edmonton as major urban centres for the province and the region were to burden those cities when boom turned to bust in the recession of 1913. In anticipation of growth, both cities had incurred enormous debts through the rapid construction of municipal services. In 1917 per capita debt reached $242 in Calgary and $359 in Edmonton. Calgary had extended municipal services over a huge area, and in some cases the sewers laid and sidewalks poured were not used until the 1950s. The widespread financial hardship experienced in Alberta in this period is indicated by the forfeiture of 43 percent of the area of the City of Edmonton to the municipal government for non-payment of taxes during the 1920s.[2]

Incipient building booms occurred in the late 1920s and the late 1930s, only to be snuffed out by the Depression and World War II respectively. Architectural development in Alberta has suffered the discontinuity of short bursts of frantic activity separated by long spells with virtually no construction. Few architects' practices weathered the mad roller coaster of boom and bust, and Alberta architecture has repeatedly suffered because its best designers have left the profession or the province when times got rough. An example of this is the story of A.M. Jeffers, the American-trained architect of the Alberta Legislative Building in Edmonton. Jeffers started his private architectural practice after brief stints as Provincial, then City Architect. The post-World War I recession meant grim times even for an architect of his prestige and experience. Like most who left Alberta, he headed west, first to Prince Rupert, then to California, where he died in 1926.[3] The existing climate of conservatism in Alberta architecture is exaggerated when no architects save those with the best family and political connections survive when boom turns to bust.

In the mid-1920s, some new notions of architectural style and design began to emerge. While not yet

A red brick house with sandstone Ionic columns, Medicine Hat, built circa 1905.

Perspective sketch for Foster McGarvey Funeral Home by Rule Wynn and Rule, 1938. Canadian Architectural Archives, The University of Calgary Library.

Tudor Period Revival house, Edmonton, late 1930s. Provincial Archives of Alberta.

Modern architecture as such, these new ideas did widen the palette of layouts, materials, and decoration available to Alberta builders. Perhaps growing out of the pervasive visual influence of the movies, or the growing connections between Alberta and the west coast, some Spanish Colonial Revival style gas stations, supermarkets, apartment houses, and even a funeral home were erected in Edmonton. The Spanish and Georgian style alternatives offered by the Edmonton firm of Rule Wynn and Rule for the Foster McGarvey Funeral Home are representative of the eclecticism of the era. The records of the Alberta Association of Architects (AAA) show at least one member listing his address in California throughout the 1920s.[4] Like the Mount Royal and Capitol Hill areas of Calgary, the Garneau and Glenora districts of Edmonton were home to a variety of architectural essays in period revival bungalow homes. Surviving houses included many using picturesque ideas of composition and materials, including a round-eaved corner bungalow reminiscent of the domestic work of English architect Philip Webb. Also found in these neighbourhoods are some meekly Tudor and Bavarian houses, and some early Moderne houses and apartment blocks.

The Stucco Vernacular architecture of Alberta of the 1920s and 1930s curiously parallels the revolutionary design ideas then brewing in Europe.[5] These planar, whitewashed, round-cornered stucco houses and commercial buildings were built most often in those areas of both rural and urban Alberta with large central or eastern European populations. While these simple buildings were being constructed in Alberta, Modern architecture was becoming firmly entrenched in Europe, particularly in Germany. While the stucco architecture of J.J.P. Oud in The Netherlands, Marcel Breuer in Germany, or Richard Neutra in Los Angeles arose out of formal aesthetic notions of the ''modernity'' of this material, the stucco architecture of Alberta could perhaps be seen as an adaptation of a vernacular building pattern from eastern or southern Europe. In a

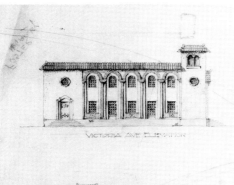

VICTORIA AVE ELEVATION

105/STREET ELEVATION

A SPANISH SOLUTION FOR FOSTER-McGARVEY

Edmonton architects Rule Wynn and Rule made this study in Spanish Colonial Revival Style for Foster McGarvey Funeral Home in 1938. Canadian Architectural Archives, The University of Calgary Library.

Safeway Stores, a company based in Oakland, California, incorporated Spanish Colonial Revival elements into early Alberta grocery outlets. This store in Edmonton's Norwood district is still in use as a corner grocery. Glenbow-Alberta Institute, Calgary.

Stucco Vernacular architecture in Calmar, Alberta, circa 1937.

recent study, John Lehr describes the wattle and daub method of applying a stucco-like surface to early Ukrainian housing in Alberta.[6] While this technique lost favour among later Ukrainian immigrants, it may have moved instead to the main streets of nearby towns and cities where stucco on chicken wire and lathe forming was used to "modernize" earlier wooden commercial buildings. The stucco building idiom of Alberta towns such as Calmar, Thorsby, or Smoky Lake gives them an architectural character quite different from earlier towns populated largely by British, American or eastern Canadian settlers. Part of the richness of Alberta architecture lies in the different building traditions and technologies used by builders in one of the most ethnically diverse rural regions of North America.

The New Thorsby Theatre of 1940 featured Stucco Vernacular architecture.

Stucco Vernacular architecture, Smoky Lake, Alberta.

The Bridgeland and Renfrew neighbourhoods of northeast Calgary became the first home to waves of eastern European immigrants and also the location of many Stucco Vernacular buildings. A prime example of these is a tiny Moderne style house on Eighth Avenue NE in Calgary in an area once known as "Germanstown." This modest house features a flat roof with overhanging eave, rounded corners, and black stripes and window trim contrasting with the stucco construction. A search of Calgary City Directories has revealed the first entry for this address in the year 1944 listing an occupant with a Germanic name and the occupation of labourer.

The use of curved corner glass, modified ribbon windows, and inset glass blocks in Calgary and Edmonton buildings of the period from 1925 to 1945 seems to indicate that the German and Dutch immigrant craftsmen who built many of them may have seen early examples of Modern architecture in Europe. These Alberta craftsmen of central or eastern European extraction were among the first to embrace elements of what would become a revolutionary new style.

Most important to the nurturing of the new architecture was the widespread publication of designs for and illustrations of "modern" streamlined houses, in various builders' and home magazines of the 1930s. Since the rise of the illustrated magazine in the nineteenth century, new ideas in housing design have often spread faster through the popular press than they have through media oriented to design professionals. With their progressive imagery of streamlined cars, ocean liners and airplanes, Hollywood movies and such mass magazines as *Look* and *Life* probably did more to foster the rise of Modern architecture than did any of Le Corbusier's polemical writings.

The 1930s and 1940s saw the rise of the streamline movement, which spread to all aspects of industrial and architectural design through advertising and the popular media. Saskatoon Public Library.

Stucco Vernacular house, Calgary, circa 1944.

"La maison d'aujourd'hui," created by French architect M. René Cera, was erected inside the T. Eaton Company store in Calgary.

This phenomenon is brought home by the boldly modern demonstration house published in *Canadian Homes and Gardens* in June 1929.[7] The house was designed by French architect and "exponent of modern decoration" M. René Cera and constructed *within* the Calgary T. Eaton store, just opened in its present building on Eighth Avenue SW. Cera called his ensemble "la maison d'aujourd'hui" and quite obviously cribbed his planar-walled and square-windowed house from Le Corbusier's villa of the mid-1920s. Mary-Etta MacPherson delicately described the effect of the project this way:

> To eyes unaccustomed to the eliminative lines, dimensions and ensemble effects of the new art, the results of M. Cera's months of observation and effort, . . . may seem strange and sudden. There is a possible bareness in the plain, flat walls, bereft of door or window frames; the old-fashioned 'cosiness' is missing, although most of the furniture is undeniably comfortable and usable.[8]

Among the furniture selected was a streamlined breakfast nook which would look appropriate in a café of the 1940s or a "retro aesthetic" bistro of the 1980s. Equipped with the latest in electric appliances, the mock home boasted round-cornered tables and dressers and an original Lawren Harris painting in the living room. While this was going on in the popular design press, the staid Royal Architectural Institute of Canada (RAIC) *Journal* was filled with illustrations of the homey High Anglicism favoured by Canada's established élite and architects, such projects as Sproatt and Rolph's Hart House at the University of Toronto, or Ridley College Chapel in St. Catharines.

The Brekke house in Ponoka, a superbly maintained example of craftsman Moderne, was built in 1942 by a carpenter owner inspired by an example in a magazine. Mr. Brekke boasts that he "has never had a problem with a flat roof"—more than could be said by many of the owners of boxy houses built in the 1930s and

1940s. Mr. Brekke's charming design is complemented by one of the few examples in Alberta of Moderne landscape design—box hedges and ribbon flower beds projecting into the front and back yards.

The Brekke House in Ponoka, built in 1942. The builder was inspired by a magazine illustration.

While these humble houses and commercial buildings spoke of things to come in street language, public buildings designed by architects reiterated a stuffy Victorian argot. It is surprising to learn that buildings such as the Red Deer Court House (1932), Banff Park Administration Building (1935), Corbett Hall, Edmonton (1929), or Edmonton's Carnegie Library (1923), were actually constructed in the 1920s and 1930s, as their decoration, detailing and plans allude to an architecture current elsewhere in North America several decades earlier. Because of the permanency of imagery and symbolism that they demand, various levels of government are renowned for holding onto architectural styles which both the market and the public perceive to be eclipsed. For example, Corbett Hall, by architect George MacDonald, is by any standard a very handsome and well-detailed Edwardian building, except that its late date of construction makes it something of an anachronism. The careful location of this building at the end of the Whyte Avenue visual axis makes it one of the best remaining examples of City Beautiful planning in the province. It was built, however, decades after the height of City Beautiful's popularity in eastern Canada and the United States. The time lag between the development of design ideas in the metropoles and the construction of imitations in Alberta diminished with every decade, but was still significant into the 1940s.

The City Beautiful Movement, inspired originally by American architects trained at the Ecole des Beaux Arts in Paris, was an urban design theory that enjoyed much public favour in the first decades of this century. The City Beautiful Movement emphasized formal, axial urban planning, with the careful management of vistas and landmarks. Minneapolis landscape architects Morrell and Nicholls prepared a plan for Edmonton which would have made the capital a Paris-like metropolis of boulevards and formal squares. Similarly, English landscape architect Thomas Mawson prepared a superb City Beautiful plan for Calgary's Civic Centre in 1914. Perhaps it is indicative of subsequent attitudes in Alberta towards such grandiose urban schemes that many of the large-scale watercolour renderings of Mawson's plan were found insulating the walls of a Calgary garage. Careful restoration of the drawings led to a major show and lecture series on Mawson's plan at Fort Calgary in 1978. None of Mawson's plan was

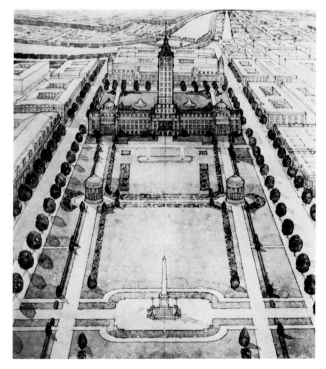

Proposed City Hall, Civic Centre Plan, Edmonton, by Minneapolis landscape architects Morrell and Nicholls. Glenbow-Alberta Institute, Calgary.

constructed but it remains a compelling image of an Alberta that might have been.

The Banff Park Administration Building of 1935, by architect Harold C. Beckett, shows that the provincial government was not alone in this conservatism of style. The axial location of this federal building at the terminus of Banff Avenue is also an example of the City Beautiful plan Mawson produced for Banff, while the building's details and form refer to a stripped-down collegiate Gothic style then popular in Toronto and the eastern United States. As in Calgary, virtually nothing else was constructed according to Mawson's plan. Moreover, Alberta was not alone in this architectural conservatism. Examples exist in Toronto of Neo-classical banks and late Gothic Revival churches conceived in the 1950s when these styles were virtually extinct in other major cities in the western world.

In the 1930s the federal government constructed a public building in Calgary featuring an Ionic entrance porch surrounded by a blocky office building. This clumsy, inelegant building is inspired less by Modern architecture than by contemporary structures erected by the federal Department of Public Works in Winnipeg, Regina and London as Depression make-work projects. A recent consultant's report has called this building a "third rate example of Colonial Architecture."[9] While this judgement by a British theatre consultant may be somewhat harsh in the Alberta context, it does point out the stylistic problems in this transitional period. By way of contrast, American federal buildings constructed in the 1930s and 1940s within the Works Progress Administration (WPA) employment programme, part of President Franklin D. Roosevelt's New Deal, adopted a very modern, streamlined style even more pronounced than it is in the Winnipeg and London federal buildings. These Depression-era streamlined structures were so common that the Moderne style is sometimes called the "WPA Style" in the United States.

It was not only in public buildings that evidence of this

The Calgary Public Building features an Ionic entrance porch.

stylistic backward glance could be found. Many of the best examples of religious architecture in Alberta consciously hearken back to older building traditions. The motives causing religious organizations to retain traditional architectural styles are, of course, different from those of governments. The reference in building forms and decoration to previous architectural traditions serves to strengthen religious and ethnic identity in a pluralist society. One only wishes that the simple yet eloquent reference to earlier religious building patterns evident in Alberta before World War II could be continued today. A drive through the southern suburbs of Lethbridge today reveals a Pentecostal meeting hall, a Catholic church, and a Buddhist temple that are virtually identical in their concrete block construction, form, and detailing, architecture seemingly having lost its power to contain and express distinctive religious sentiment.

The Calgary Public Building, built by the Canadian government in the 1930s.

In the period from 1920 to 1950 a number of architecturally significant religious buildings were produced. Foremost among these was the Al Raschid Mosque in Edmonton, now generally recognized as the first purpose-built mosque in North America.[10] The Al Raschid is a relatively modest structure originally constructed in 1937 in wood frame on property near 101 Street and 108 Avenue. When Edmonton's Public School Board decided to construct its vocational school on the site in 1946, the Moslem community agreed to move the mosque four blocks north to where it now stands, near the Royal Alexandra Hospital. This created something of an architectural and religious problem in that the niche directed towards Mecca, or the mihrab, now faced the opposite direction. However, an enterprising and pragmatic mullah, or prayer leader, realized in the 1960s that the shortest route from Edmonton to Mecca was a great circle route northeast over the pole, so the mihrab could stay where it was.

The Al Raschid Mosque, constructed in 1937, was moved to its current site at 101 Street and 112 Avenue, Edmonton, in 1946. Provincial Archives of Alberta.

The building is from the Turkish tradition of mosque design, the most similar among mosque architectural traditions to western church layouts in plan. The distinctively Islamic architectural features of the building including the mihrab, some geometrically decorated hardware and light fixtures, the glazing and voussoir patterns of the windows, and hammered metal twin domes at the entrance end. The building uses standard Canadian wood frame construction techniques from the period, with a gable roof and typical floor and roof joint detailing. The Al Raschid Mosque stands as a tribute to the vision and determination of Alberta's early Moslem community, all the more notable for being the first building of its type constructed on this half of the globe.

Near the end of the Depression, Edmonton's Ukrainian Catholic community began construction of a long-awaited major church. St. Josaphat's Ukrainian Catholic Cathedral in Edmonton, constructed between 1937 and 1947, is a building in which the meticulous procedures of traditional construction were chosen over the expediencies of steel reinforcement and pre-made components. The church has a typical Byzantine cross plan, with an elaborate attached Greek porch in, strangely, a modified Tuscan order. The polychrome

St. Josaphat's Ukrainian Catholic Cathedral, Edmonton, was constructed between 1937 and 1947. Architect the Reverend Ruh based his plan on St. Sophia's Cathedral, Kiev. Photograph by Gary Chen, Historic Sites Service, Alberta Culture.

brick patterning and massing configuration of the domes is particularly successful. The building was designed by the Austrian-trained Reverend Philip Ruh, who based his plans on St. Sophia in Kiev, the mother church for Ukrainians. The Reverend Ruh also designed the Ukrainian Catholic church in Crooks Creek, Manitoba. After World War II, Julian and Bohdan Bucmaniuk painted the superb Byzantine-style murals which now adorn the vaults of the nave and transepts of the cathedral. The building was constructed for a remarkable $150,000, but the inclusion of materials and labour donated by parish members would easily triple its real cost. The product of a long labour of love for Edmonton's Ukrainian Catholic community, the church demonstrates a striking urban presence.[11] In both the Al Raschid Mosque and St. Josaphat's Cathedral, centuries-old ideas of religious architecture were adapted successfully to the modern world.

The design of the first two temples of the Church of Jesus Christ of the Latter-Day Saints (Mormon) constructed outside the continental United States employed some radical new ideas of architectural form based on the designs of Frank Lloyd Wright. The temple at Laie Oahu, Hawaii, from 1915, and the Cardston Temple, which followed it, were radically different from earlier church buildings of the Mormons. The earliest Mormon temples, those in Kirtland, Ohio, and Nauvoo, Illinois, were designed in nineteenth-century Gothic Revival and Neo-Georgian styles respectively.[12] The four main Mormon temples in Utah were done in heavy and severe Gothic style. The Mormon temple in Cardston can be described as the first consciously "Modern" major building in the history of Alberta architecture. Laurel B. Andrew, in his book *The Early Temples of the Mormons,* describes the change this way:

> The castellated Gothic [style] disappeared entirely to be replaced by a more contemporary mode echoing Frank Lloyd Wright's architecture, especially his Unity Temple [in Chicago, Illinois].

The Alberta Temple of the Church of Jesus Christ of the Latter-Day Saints (Mormons) by American architects Hyrum Pope and Harold Burton, 1913-23. H. Pollard Collection, Provincial Archives of Alberta.

Even the distinctive double-ended form was rejected, along with the multiple towers, in favour of a centralized Greek cross plan that seems to refer to the temples of the Central American Indians, which Latter-Day Saints believe to be the artifacts of the civilization chronicled in the Book of Mormon.[13]

The Cardston Temple was designed in 1913 by American architects Hyrum Pope and Harold Burton, both of whom had been exposed to Frank Lloyd Wright's work during their studies in Chicago. After nearly a decade of construction the temple was dedicated in 1923. The massing of the Cardston Temple rises magnificently above its prairie foothill setting, one

The Alberta Temple of the Church of Jesus Christ of the Latter-Day Saints at Cardston was the first consciously "Modern" major building in the province. H. Pollard Collection, Provincial Archives of Alberta.

of the most superbly sited buildings in Alberta. The stonework, the window detailing, and articulation of the modern cornice were clearly advanced in craftsmanship and design for an Alberta building of the period. The most striking Wrightian details of the temple are the chevron-patterned wrought-iron gates and leaded glass, the decorative mouldings on the window surrounds, and the oversize urns flanking each elevation. The building is faced in unpolished granite and features at its centre an octagon 118 feet in diameter and 84 feet high. The interior, which is not open to those who are not active Mormons, is from all reports bright and richly decorated, in sharp contrast to the solemn grey exterior.

Exterior view of the Banff Park Pavilion, designed by Frank Lloyd Wright and Francis Sullivan in 1911. Glenbow-Alberta Institute, Calgary.

Alberta's only building designed by Frank Lloyd Wright himself fell into disrepair and was destroyed in the late 1930s. In 1911, the federal government commissioned Wright and his associate architect from Ottawa, Francis Sullivan, to design a recreation centre, really a dance hall, for the town of Banff. Wright spent some time at the Banff Springs Hotel in 1911, seeking to escape the notoriety that his affair with a key client's wife had generated in Chicago. Connections Wright made in Banff, coupled with the links his former employee, Francis Sullivan, had to the federal Department of

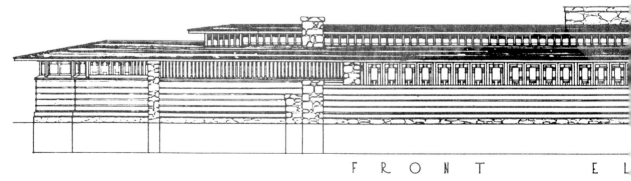

F R O N T   E L

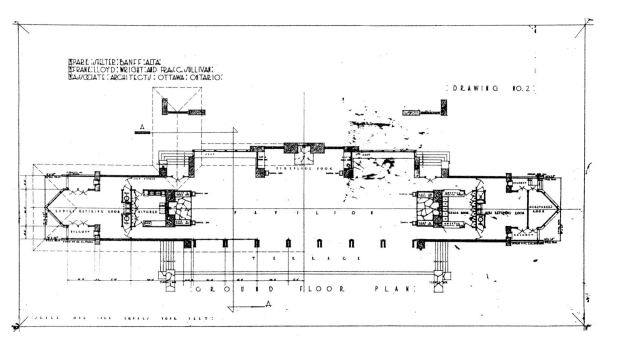

Ground floor plan, Banff Park Pavilion, 1911. Public Archives of Canada, Ottawa.

Front elevation, Frank Lloyd Wright's Banff Park Pavilion, 1911. Public Archives of Canada, Ottawa.

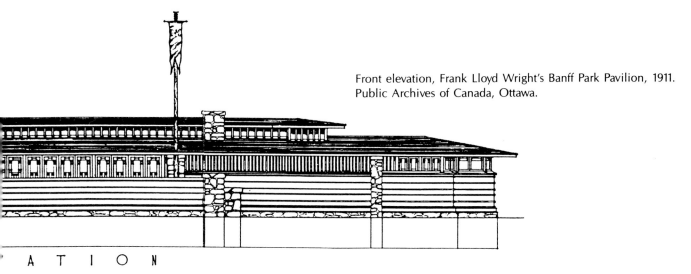

Public Works, secured Wright the Banff commission.
Wright is known to have visited the Banff construction
site en route to Japan, where he was designing Tokyo's
Imperial Hotel. The building was one of a handful of
Wright buildings constructed with a rough-sawn log
technique. Characteristically long and low,[14] the Banff
Park Pavilion featured the overhanging roof, dark brown
wood stain, and breezeway characteristic of Wright's
Oak Park period. Cut-glass leaded windows with
Wright's emblematic chevron decorated pattern were
used in the building, as were elaborate light diffusers
similar to those designed for the Martin House in
Buffalo, New York.

Wright designed unique alcove benches and other
details that showed his attention to architecture at every
scale. Old-timers, like users of Wright buildings
everywhere, remark on the tight dimensions and low
height of the benches designed by the short-statured
architect. The building was not a total success; it
would seem that Wright did not radically alter his Oak
Park house prototype for use as a dance hall, but
merely extended it. Foundations were particularly
inadequate, and in general the detailing was ill-suited
to its site. Banff residents were also annoyed by the
project, not only because Ottawa had acted unilaterally,
but also because a picnic pavilion was not what they
wanted: true blue Canadians, Banff residents wanted a
hockey arena! Some longtime residents later boasted
they had never set foot in the building, its primary
users being the Mount Royal set from Calgary who
tooled out in their roadsters to picnic and dance on
sunny Sundays.

An exposed king truss and unconcealed services in the
interior of the oddly elongated hall were as

characteristic of Wright's design as they were unusual
for the period. When Wright's work was published in
Europe by Wasmuth, his decorative approach and
functionalist directness proved influential to designers in
the applied and architectural arts. While it was a very
modest commission, the Banff building sufficiently
interested Wright that he produced a superb rendering
of the pavilion from his own hand. This drawing shows
not only Wright's mastery of axial massing in crude
materials, but also a certain idealistic naïveté about site
conditions, as this was his first building in an alpine
environment.

39

Wright's technical innovation and his pragmatic and functional approach to building plans and massing were key sources of inspiration to such early Modern architects in Europe as Walter Gropius, Peter Behrens, and H.P. Berlage. Alberta architects had only a limited chance to be influenced by the Banff Park Pavilion, which fell into disuse and was accidentally demolished by a Parks crew during the Depression. The most likely of the many apocryphal stories concerning the demolition contends that a flood of the flats area in 1938 soaked the first few timber courses of the pavilion. Then, to add architectural insult to injury, a Parks employee backed a bulldozer into the building while cutting a drainage ditch. With a corner collapsed and the rest of the structure in poor repair, the demolition job was complete before Parks officials realized what had been destroyed.

The 1930s were not good years for Alberta's historic structures. One of the original reasons for locating the Legislative Buildings adjacent to the Hudson's Bay Company Fort was to present a symbolic historical continuity. Since, however, any visual evidence of past booms seems inimical to the boomtown architectural ethos, provincial officials ordered the dismantling of Fort Edmonton several years later. When Fort Edmonton was finally torn down, portions of the Factor's House were disassembled, numbered, and stored in the basement of the Legislative Building in the hope that they might be used in a future reconstruction. The logs were mistakenly burned during a huge bonfire on the Legislative Grounds celebrating the coronation of King George VI in 1937. Only a few charred scraps remain of this last of a series of log forts which preceded the province's capital city.

The sad fate of two of Alberta's most historically and architecturally significant buildings in the 1930s indicates how ripe the province was for new notions of architectural form and design. It seemed then, and still seems today, that many Albertans seek only to forget their built past. Unlike the European modernists,

The demolition of Fort Edmonton, showing the Alberta Legislative Building in the background. Glenbow-Alberta Institute, Calgary.

Alberta architects had precious little burden of history with which to struggle.

The Eighth Avenue elevation of the Bank of Nova Scotia in Calgary, designed by Toronto architect John M. Lyle, 1930. H. Pollard Collection, Provincial Archives of Alberta.

An example of John M. Lyle's Beaux-Arts work, The Memorial Arch, Royal Military College, Kingston, Ontario, 1922. Ontario Archives, Toronto.

The transition to modernism in Alberta architecture can be seen most eloquently in the 1929 Bank of Nova Scotia building in Calgary, designed by architect John Lyle. This was Lyle's first building in western Canada after he had built a successful practice in eastern Canada. Born in Ireland in 1872, John M. Lyle grew up in Hamilton, Ontario. He took a degree from Yale University and then studied at the Ecole des Beaux–Arts in Paris like many of the most important American architects of the late nineteenth century. He returned to

A further example of John M. Lyle's work: The Bank of Nova Scotia, Ottawa. Photograph courtesy of The Bank of Nova Scotia.

Canada to interpret in a sensitive and innovative manner the Beaux Arts method of historicist architectural design. His Memorial Arch at the Royal Military College, Kingston, Ontario, designed in 1922, is one of Canada's best examples of pure Beaux–Arts architecture, an architecture which thrived on monuments, competitions and a nearly archeological sensitivity to the buildings of antiquity. He also designed Ottawa's Sparks Street branch of the Bank of Nova Scotia in 1924. This bank is approximately the same size as the Bank of Nova Scotia building in Calgary and has an analogous mid-block site in downtown Ottawa. Furthermore, the delicate symmetry of the temple-bank, the pattern and size of door and window openings, and the proportion of pilasters and cornices are virtually the same for both eastern and western banks. But with respect to architectural style, a major change occurred in the five years that elapsed between construction of the two banks: the rusticated base, recessed porch, incised metopes, and clean Doric order of the Ottawa bank set it unswervingly in the Beaux–Arts tradition of McKim, Mead and White of New York, while the Calgary bank in its severe rectilinearity and Art Deco decorative sense points to an incipient modernism.

In Canada, the Victorian tradition of the bank as a classical temple, of which both Ottawa and Calgary buildings are late representatives, lived on longer than it did in the United States or even Britain. Because of government chartered monopolies, Canada has had fewer, but richer, and more conservative banks than other western countries. The wealth and conservatism of Canadian banks was reflected, of course, in the buildings commissioned. Such a context makes the incipient modernism of the Calgary bank even more important. One need go no further than across Calgary's Eighth Avenue SW to the main branch of the

Bank of Montreal, by Montreal architect Frederick Rea (1930), to see the more dryly academic classical banks that Lyle's contemporaries produced in the second quarter of this century. The tired and stuffy detailing and decorative programme of the Bank of Montreal is as telling an example as exists in Alberta of the continually recycled historical forms to which Adolf Loos, Le Corbusier, and other pioneers of the Modern Movement in architecture objected.

Between the design of the Ottawa and the Calgary banks, Lyle made an extended visit to Europe in the late summer and autumn of 1928. In a speech before the RAIC in 1929 he explained the rationale for his trip:

> I was keen to visit my old haunts in the Latin Quarter, and to see what new buildings had been erected since last I was there, and was particularly anxious to study the Modern Movement in architecture which is now sweeping over the world. The Modern Movement has, in my opinion much to commend it. It might be described as a revolt against archeology in architecture, and while much of the work that has been done in this manner is thoroughly bad, there is also very much that is very sound and very beautiful.[15]

This address, printed in the RAIC *Journal* in 1929, is the first mention of the Modern Movement in Canada's only architectural magazine, then five years old. It is interesting that in the 1930s, when the Modern Movement became impossible to ignore for even the stodgiest of Canadian architects, it was Lyle, almost alone, who wrote positively of it.

Because of his Beaux-Arts heritage, and perhaps because of his catious Canadian temperament, Lyle did not agree with the European leaders of the Modern Movement who thought that change in architectural styles need be revolutionary:

The Bank of Montreal, Eighth Avenue, Calgary, designed by Frederick Rea, 1930, showing the Hudson's Bay Company store in the background. H. Pollard Collection, Provincial Archives of Alberta.

I do not believe that a style can be born overnight, but rather it is a gradual development with tradition as a background. The skilled designer, through the solving of modern problems, and the use and combination of new materials, should be able to strike a new and personal note.[16]

The Bank of Nova Scotia on Eighth Avenue SW in Calgary, Lyle's first major commission after his European trip, struck a new and personal note unusual in a building housing a traditional institution. In the Calgary bank, a special type of chemistry seems to have guided Lyle in this reconciliation of modelled classical front with flattened modernism, and Art Deco pattern-making with locally inspired sculpture. As the building faces north and is in shade much of the year, many Calgarians pass the building by, barely noticing the complex symbolic system Lyle concocted to represent visually the Alberta of the 1920s.

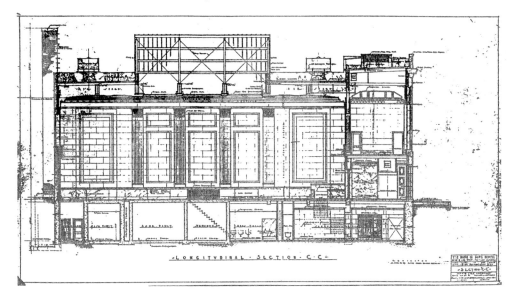

Bank of Nova Scotia, Calgary. A longitudinal section.
Canadian Architectural Archives, Stevenson Raines Collection, The University of Calgary Library.

The Bank of Nova Scotia fronts onto Eighth Avenue SW, the city's main shopping street, and a pedestrian mall. The building measures 50 by 115 feet by 35 feet high, with the airy and boxy banking hall taking up the bulk of this volume. The bank hall boasts flat pilasters with incised reeding instead of fluting; along with many other uses of natural forms throughout the building, this was intended to indicate the bountiful living wealth of the prairies. By way of contrast, the capitals of these interior pilasters incorporate anvils and gear wheels symbolizing the emerging industrial power of the new west. Even more bizarre are the capitals of the exterior pilasters which incorporate a spread-winged eagle and a stylized spring from a Model "A" Ford.

Art Deco lamps decorate the building, while the bronze window grilles continue the symbolism of this remarkable building. Decoration here includes the thistle, the shamrock, the leek, the rose, the fleur-de-lis, and the maple leaf representative of the Scottish, Irish, Welsh, English, and French ethnic traditions which, in the eyes of the architect, represented the foundations of Canada. The banking hall is lit by a huge skylight that also features decorations employing organic forms. The remaining portions of the ceiling are covered by moulded gold-leaf patterns similar to those in the Ottawa bank and the ceiling treatment of the great ticket hall of Union Station in Toronto, of which Lyle was a principal designer.

Despite the extensive decoration and classical language of the pilasters, this is not a traditional Victorian banking hall. The flatness of the wall treatment, the hard rectilinearity of the room, and the verticality enforced by the dramatic lighting and light colours are indicators of its early modernism. The result of the decoration, forms, and spaces of the building is what a contemporary account calls "an atmosphere of rest and affluence."[17]

It is in the sculpted street elevation of the building that Lyle's modernism is most evident. The steel structure of

Art Deco lamps decorate the walls at the pedestrian level. The windows are framed with symbols of the Old West including a buffalo, an Indian, a Mountie, and a horse.

the bank relieves the limestone front from bearing loads, allowing the façade to become more reminiscent of a prairie boomtown front than any eastern banking temple. Lyle enforces this by employing a highly visible free-standing parapet for a building on a Calgary street which, even today, has some vestigial false fronts. The pilasters are modelled just enough so that they can be read; they are remnants of an earlier tradition, here exploited only for the air of permanence and stability their associations lend. Lyle retreated from a complete break with the classical architectural language of the orders, but rephrased them in a light, jazzy syncopation.

Linked to this restatement of the classical idiom is the architect's use of local visual symbols in the sculptural programme that runs throughout. Lyle's Calgary bank is one of the most visually stunning reconciliations of architectural regionalism with nationalism in Canadian history. The splayed window on the main floor reveals sculpted square-jawed Mounties and feathered Indians surrounded by horses, buffalo, guns, and arrows in celebration of the Old West before and after the arrival of the white man. The main architrave features wild flowers of the prairies, along with inverted triangle shapes which read to the modern eye as Art Deco decoration but were justified by the architect to his pin-striped clients as a traditional Indian symbol of progress. The window surrounds are lightly incised, but evidently owe more to contemporary Moderne than historical Mannerism.

The size and blockiness of the dentils also merge the employed classical idiom with the emerging rectilinear design ideas of the Modern Movement. In this, Lyle may have responded to his own interpretation of the Modern architecture he saw in Europe in 1928:

> The characteristics of the new movement are a simplicity of wall surface, both of exterior and interior, a use of parallel lines or concentric curves, a use of incised relief ornament with semi-

The main architrave features prairie flowers.

flat surfaces, a daring use of modern materials such as the combinations of metal and glass, wood and metal, an altogether charming use of what might be termed sunshine colours, their interiors being keyed to a lighter, gayer note.[18]

The lower string course features an Indian dogtooth pattern while the cornice utilizes a water leaf pattern, but both are firmly within the Art Deco tradition of applied architectural decoration.

One decorative panel shows a wheat sheaf in front of an Art Deco prairie sunset.

Another panel shows a saddle on a fence and below it the bronze window grilles depict the fleur-de-lis and the shamrock.

The panel over the central window features a wheat sheaf in front of the prairie sun setting in radiant Art Deco splendour. The panel to its right features a saddle on an undulating fence with the Rockies shimmering in the background. The last and most prescient of Lyle's depictions of the economic engines of the Alberta of the 1920s is an oil rig gushing like a ragtime Fontainebleau. Lyle designed the bank some years after the relatively minor oil discovery at Turner Valley, when the province's later oil riches were inconceivable. Lyle's elaborate taxonomy of natural and economic symbols is a passionate attempt to give a humane and familiar face to a national institution frequently resented by westerners—the bank. He mounted his regional symbolic system on light-coloured, planar walls inspired

A third panel symbolizes the promise of western oil.

by the rising tide of the European Modern Movement in architecture.

Lyle and his sculptor showed a sensitivity to the visual power of local symbols. Only the Marine (1931) and the Medical-Dental (1930) buildings in Vancouver by McCarter and Nairne, Lyle's subsequent Runnymede Branch Library, Toronto (1931), and his head office building for the Bank of Nova Scotia in Halifax (1937) come close to the Calgary bank for eloquence of decorative regionalism in Canadian architecture. A few years after the completion of the building, Lyle explained in an article in *The Canadian Banker* that the intent in the Calgary building was to present a local face for a traditionally imposing national institution.[19] It is much credit to Lyle's talents as an architect that he was able to convince a client like a major bank to engage in the fun-filled playing with symbols and architectural tradition that one sees in this building. Lyle's local allusions in the sculptural programme of the contemporary Sparks Street, Ottawa, Bank of Nova Scotia are much more restrained, while the interior gilt is much richer, perhaps an accurate architectural depiction of Canadian regional differences in this period. The Calgary bank itself occupied the building as a regional head office until 1976, when it moved into new quarters in Scotia Square. The building has recently been declared one of the first post-1925 Alberta Historic Resources, and has gained a new lease on life as a discothèque.

The 1920s and 1930s in Alberta architecture saw an increasing variance in design approaches, a pluralism of architectural styles. The Lyle bank, and the religious and vernacular buildings described in this chapter were all still part of a widening of Victorian rather than truly Modernist architectural sensibilities. While many of the vernacular buildings illustrated here contain elements of an emergent modernism, they had surprisingly little impact on the work of architects, who recognized only loftier sources of ideas. Parallel to the widespread appreciation—but negligible built impact—of Frank Lloyd Wright's non-domestic designs across the continent, Alberta boasted two superb Wrightian buildings which sparked no further architectural explorations in the same mode.

In his seminal study of the sociology of ideas, Thomas Kuhn describes a troubled period when an existing scientific paradigm is attacked for its inadequacies in accounting for data, but is nonetheless maintained, until a new and more inclusive paradigm arises to take its place.[20] Kuhn's musings on the periods of fundamental conceptual change in the physical sciences, such as the Copernican, Newtonian, or Einsteinian scientific revolutions, have at least a superficial application to the situation in Canadian architecture in this period. While the social, aesthetic, economic, and technological phenomena that had given rise to Victorian historicist architecture had changed by the second quarter of the twentieth century, the buildings which served as their shells, reflections, and emblems had not. What was lacking was a new paradigm of what architecture could or should be. That paradigm was already emerging in Europe.

The Administration Building (right), and the Hall of Machines (left) at the Werkbund Exposition, Cologne, Germany, designed by Walter Gropius and Adolph Meyer in 1914. Photograph courtesy of The Museum of Modern Art, New York.

SOURCES OF MODERNISM

The winds of fundamental change in architectural design were blowing from Europe to all parts of the western world in the 1920s. Even an area as isolated as Alberta would see the theoretical and practical basis of its architecture drastically altered during the succeeding two decades. The beginnings of the Modern Movement in architecture were tied up in an international exchange of ideas, the likes of which architecture had seldom seen before. The Deutscher Werkbund Group in Germany built upon the ideas of the English Arts and Crafts Movement, but went further to accept the design implications of industrial labour and production. They and the modernists who followed them acknowledged the brilliance and innovation of Frank Lloyd Wright and his mentor Louis Sullivan, but the Europeans' admiration focussed more on the Americans' radical theoretical pose and technical innovation than it did on their architectural forms. The commitment of both designers to ornament was widely ignored in the heat of the theoretical battles of the 'teens and twenties. Wright was to become one of the most admired but least imitated architects of the twentieth century. The Deutscher Werkbund architects were among the first to attempt a radically new architectural treatment for industrial buildings. Peter Behrens's 1909 AEG (General Electricity Company) Turbine Factory in Berlin would prove to be among the most influential, especially for

The most notable technical innovation at the Fagus Factory was the glazed corner. Photograph courtesy of The Museum of Modern Art, New York.

employees in his architectural firm who went on to form the core of the Modern Movement: Walter Gropius, Mies van der Rohe, and, for a brief period, Charles–Edouard Jeanneret–Gris.[1]

Nearly as influential was a pre-World War I factory with a boldly exhibited expression of building components and the frank use of steel and glass. The Fagus Factory by Walter Gropius, in association with Adolph Meyer, prefigured the rise of both the structural rationalism and the industrial aesthetic of much of Modern architecture. Its most famous innovation was the glazed corner where, because of the internal structure and cantilever, glass could be substituted for bearing steel or brick. While this portion of the building was revolutionary, the seldom published rear was much nearer to the mainstream of Werkbund architecture.

The Fagus Factory, Alfeld-an-der-Leine, Germany, by Walter Gropius, in association with Adolph Meyer, 1910-14. Photograph courtesy of The Museum of Modern Art, New York.

A view from the north of the Villa Savoye at Poissy-sur-Seine, France, by Le Corbusier, 1929-30. Photograph courtesy of The Museum of Modern Art, New York.

Charles-Edouard Jeanneret-Gris began a serious career as an architect in his mid-thirties after several years of dabbling in other artistic pursuits. He had designed several regionalist houses in his home town of La Chaux-de-Fonds in Switzerland, had worked briefly for Auguste Perret and other leading architects, and travelled extensively through the Middle East. After establishing himself as a "purist" painter (see page 17) of some repute, he published, in conjunction with Amédée Ozenfant and Paul Dermée, *L'Esprit Nouveau,* a magazine of inter-arts criticism. He adopted a professional name modelled after a distant relative, Le Corbusier. As much through his prolific and polemical writings as through his building designs, he became the linchpin, the hinge and the hub of Modern architecture. One of its few enduring geniuses, in such late projects as the chapel at Ronchamp or the Dominican Friary of La Tourette, Le Corbusier also became one of Modern

The Villa Jeanneret, La Chaux-de-Fonds, Switzerland, by Le Corbusier, 1911. Photograph courtesy of The Museum of Modern Art, New York.

architecture's earliest and most eloquent critics and revisionists.

With the encouragement of Wilhelm-Ernst, Grand-duc de Saxe-Weimar-Eisenach, Walter Gropius combined the Weimar Art Academy with the Arts and Crafts school[2] to form the Bauhaus School of Design in Weimar in 1919. In 1925, the Bauhaus moved to a stunning new building in Dessau designed by Gropius. The building was a crystalline expression of the philosophy and curriculum Gropius had developed for the Bauhaus: the building was extremely efficient in plan and massing, with the different school functions clearly expressed in form. It used the latest in steel and glass technology to bring together education, living, and playing in one strong architectural expression: its interior and furniture were generated by principles analogous to the building design; indeed, many of the workshop interiors were designed by workshop members themselves. This institution was to do more than any other body to promote the new design sensibility.

The Bauhaus was far more than a school of architecture, as it trained students in all the visual and applied arts. Moreover, it employed a methodically sequenced visual education built around what amounted to a general theory of design. At the core of the Bauhaus system of education, and of much of Modern architecture which followed it, was the somewhat unwieldy German concept of *Gesamtkunstwerk*. This has been popularized by the inadequate English phrase "Total Design"; but "life as a total work of art," with its resonance to the music-dramas of Richard Wagner, who promoted the term, might be more indicative of the intentions of Meyer and Gropius. At its simplest, the idea meant that all aspects of human tools and environment should be completely designed by reducing each part to its functional, elementary components, all too often understood literally as simple geometric forms. This architectural Platonism had much to do with the rise of the notion

The Bauhaus School of Design, by Walter Gropius, trained students in all the visual and applied arts. Photograph courtesy of The Museum of Modern Art, New York.

A key institution and design in the evolution of Modern architecture: The Bauhaus School, Dessau, Germany, by Walter Gropius, 1925-26. Photograph courtesy of The Museum of Modern Art, New York.

of the hero-architect, leaping from history to heal human ills with reason and the right angle.[3]

The rise of Naziism in the thirties forced Walter Gropius to join fellow German and Austrian designers Ludwig Mies van der Rohe, Marcel Breuer, Richard Neutra, and Richard Schindler in the United States. The first three of these men came to dominate key architecture schools, and, through their leadership and the publication of their work, they helped establish Modern architecture in North America. Mies taught at the Illinois Institute of Technology, Gropius at Harvard and the Massachusetts Institute of Technology. Neutra

Le Corbusier was impressed by the unfettered functionalism implicit in the shape of Canadian grain-handling buildings. A photograph of this Calgary grain elevator appeared in Le Corbusier's book, *Vers Une Architecture*. H. Pollard Collection, Provincial Archives of Alberta.

and Schindler both practiced in Southern California, and, while less academically oriented than the others, had considerable impact on the west.[4] Disciples of both Mies and Gropius came to Canadian architecture schools, especially to the University of Manitoba, where prominent Canadian architects such as John C. Parkin were trained in the new style starting in the mid-1930s. Under the guidance of John Russell, an American student of Gropius, the architecture school in Winnipeg helped complete the conversion of prairie architecture to the International Style. By 1950, variations of Bauhaus architectural teachings were installed virtually everywhere, with the odd pockets of Beaux-Arts resistance such as the University of Pennsylvania or Yale University. Interestingly, these universities became birthplaces of Post-Modern architecture through the efforts of Louis Kahn, Robert Venturi, Robert Stern, Charles Moore, and others.

The flow of ideas was not exclusively westward across the Atlantic during the twenties. In a book that more than any other was to change the shape of this century's architecture, *Vers Une Architecture* (published in English as *Towards a New Architecture*), Le Corbusier glowingly described as key sources for a new, distinctly twentieth-century architecture, such honestly expressed North American engineering structures as Model "T" motor cars and Canadian grain elevators.[5] Along with grain terminals in Montreal and Thunder Bay, Le Corbusier included a photograph of the Canadian government grain elevator in Calgary, calling them the "first fruits of the new era" of modernism. Le Corbusier had received a packet of promotional photographs of Canadian grain-handling buildings from Walter Gropius that so impressed him that he published the group in the chapter of his book dealing with the "engineers aesthetic." Both men were impressed with the development of efficient slip-cast concrete technologies and the unfettered functionalism implicit in the shapes of these buildings. The main federal elevator in southeast Calgary[6] was to remain the most internationally renowned piece of Alberta architecture until the widespread publication of designs for the Edmonton Housing Union Building (HUB) by Barton Myers, Jack Diamond, and Richard L. Wilkin nearly fifty years later.

The work of two architectural critics, Henry-Russell Hitchcock Jr. and Philip Johnson, helped formally to introduce the new European architecture to North America. The publication of Hitchcock's *Modern Architecture*,[7] followed by Hitchcock and Johnson's *The International Style*[8] with an accompanying show at the Museum of Modern Art in New York, helped entrench the new architectural style on this continent when only a handful of such buildings had been completed in North America. In his introduction to the Modern Architecture Show at the Museum of Modern Art in 1931, Henry-Russell Hitchcock Jr. carefully distinguished between the true modern International Style architecture of the Europeans, and the "modernistic" designs of Americans of the 1920s and 1930s. This narrow view, understandable in the polemical phase in the establishment of a new style, has led several generations of architects and critics to hold in disdain such "modernistic" buildings as stucco houses, service stations, or movie theatres. With a growing critical perspective on the birth and growth of Modern architecture in recent years, the "modernistic" designs of North America only now are being held in higher regard. These designs are generally described by two terms appropriated from France in the 1920s: Art Deco and Art Moderne.[9] While the show got no closer to Canada than Buffalo, widespread coverage in the professional and general press assured attention even in the depths of a major depression. The characteristics of these and other twentieth-century architectural styles are described in the Appendix, "A Sampler of Modern Styles."

It was in the uniquely twentieth-century building types of the cinema, the utility structure, and the service station, that the functional, fervently anti-historical

European Modern Movement ideas first made their presence known in the architecture of English-speaking countries. It is important to note here that these building types had no architectural tradition to build upon, except obliquely from the theatre to the cinema, and from the livery stable to the service station. Moreover, the associations of these building types with the new transportation and communications technologies made them naturals for experimentation with Modern Movement ideas, however misquoted and misunderstood they were initially. For example, the Centenary Exhibition of the Royal Institute of British Architects in 1934 seemed professionally and polemically predisposed against Modern architecture. While the gallery show contained photos of the Villa Savoye by Le Corbusier and Wiessenhofsiedlung Housing by Gropius, the only two examples of Modern architecture actually illustrated in the exhibition's catalogue were a Shell service station and a London cinema. The compilers of the catalogue, who included some of Britain's leading architects, apparently could accept the notion of a new style for these two building types, but not for housing.

Canada's architectural elite were no more disposed to the new style than their British counterparts. John Lyle was the only person to mention Modern architecture in the pages of the RAIC *Journal* between its inception in 1924 and the end of the decade. The pages of the *Journal* during this period were full of Gothic Revival and Beaux-Arts buildings, out-of-place anachronisms even then. The Canadian architectural profession and schools were particularly slow to come to terms with modernism, giving strong credence that Modern architecture percolated up from popular culture, rather than down from the visions of the Academy.

The earliest service stations were mere outgrowths of livery stables, with little thought given to gasoline storage and pumping. After 1920, purpose-designed buildings began to appear, usually with small buildings connected to a row of pumps by a breezeway. Like the

A Richfield Service Station in Calgary's Hillhurst district, built circa 1920. H. Pollard Collection, Provincial Archives of Alberta.

example from Calgary's Hillhurst district of the 1920s, they were generally done in vague and stripped-down versions of historicist revival styles. While this building employed Spanish elements, others employed Tudor, Picturesque, or even Chinese imagery. By the late 1920s, white streamlined service stations had begun to appear, beginning a tradition of Modernism in these buildings that lasted until the 1960s, when historical and rustic styles reappeared.

Two Calgary Texaco service stations, constructed in 1928 and 1929, were remarkable for the radical break they made with Alberta architecture of the period.[10] The planar, streamlined forms of these stations showed a distinct currency with continental notions of the machine aesthetic, while at the same time accomplishing their humble functions of servicing and refuelling cars.

The Big Chief Service Station on Seventeenth Avenue South in Calgary was of stucco and wood frame construction. With the rising prices of more traditional clapboard construction, stucco became an important building material after World War I, especially in northern Alberta where it still forms something of a regional vernacular architecture. The Big Chief was the first Calgary service station designed to include a café, the first such combination in the city. Stucco, plywood forming and chicken wire mesh made the Moderne rounded corners and smooth white surfaces possible, even desirable. With hardly a flat surface on the entire front façade of the building, the Big Chief Service Station was a study in the use of this technique. The building was perhaps most remarkable for its fanciful sign tower designed by the Texaco architects to accommodate the company's big red star.

The raised, horizontal painted cornice banding, referred to during the period affectionately as "speed whiskers," carried the Texaco corporate presence to all corners of the building, and greatly emphasized the horizontal nature of the structure. This was further enhanced by

The Big Chief Service Station, Calgary, built circa 1929.

The Big Chief Service Station was most notable for its fanciful sign tower.

Interior detail in a Texaco service station.
Provincial Archives of Alberta.

The Red Indian Service Station, Calgary, built circa 1929.

the use of the common Modern Movement detail of industrial sash windows with horizontal mullions. These window mullions imposed a rectilinear order on views in a period when plate glass or standard sash windows were readily and cheaply available. The Texaco "Total Design" was carried even to the tool shelves of the service areas, which were streamlined in appearance to complete the effect. It is one of the basic tenets of Modern design that a continuity of design forms be employed from the tiniest implement or piece of furniture, to the massing of the entire building. This building thus showed a number of the visual characteristics of the Modern Movement in the elements of form it employed to demonstrate the progressive nature of the service station. The Big Chief Service Station was gutted by fire, then demolished in 1980.

The Red Indian Service Station on Centre Street in Calgary was a smaller but similar Texaco station of the same period. Once again, much of the building was but a pretext for the sign tower, which had a stepped back, almost ziggurat form. The use of "speed whiskers" here was particularly interesting, and the proportions of the sign towers and spacing of the window mullions were carefully and artfully considered. The massing and curvilinear forms of this service station harkened back to German Expressionist architecture, especially the Einstein Tower by Erich Mendelsohn (see page 96). They also strangely prefigured the forms of Edmonton architect Douglas Cardinal, whose work is discussed in chapter 4. The Red Indian Service Station was used by a dairy company in the 1970s but was demolished in 1977 to make way for an office building.

Despite the loss of both these prime urban examples of streamlined Moderne service station architecture, a delightfully bizarre example of this architecture still stands in southern Alberta. The town of Raymond, near Lethbridge, built an indoor arena with an ornate south façade in the 1920s. When a service station was built next door in the 1940s, it responded, in white curving stucco, to every dip and rise of the town building, and then some. The two buildings still stand, as if engaged in an argument between the Jazz-Age Baroque of the arena and the Rococo Moderne of the service station. It would seem that the latter is winning, as the roof of the arena has started to sag, its ridge beam beginning to match the lines of the front façade.

Leaving the forbidden pleasures of vernacular Moderne architecture, the conversion from late Victorian architecture to self-conscious, high style Modern architecture can be seen in the career of one architect, Peter Rule. Rule arrived in Edmonton from England shortly before World War I. He worked for a prominent Edmonton firm, Magoon and MacDonald, but like so many others in Alberta's barely established design and construction industries, was called to serve in Europe during the war. On his return he found that the pre-war building boom had ended, imposing painful adjustments on architects. Over-construction, resulting from land and building speculation during the boom, made life even more difficult for young architects in the early twenties. Rule soon took a job with Alberta Government Telephones (AGT) as architect, although the official title of his position was Building Inspector. He remained with the company for nearly twenty years before going on to guide the formation of an architectural firm critical to the development of Modern architecture in Alberta.

Rule's first buildings for AGT were traditional brick structures, as appropriate to his native England as to the tiny Alberta towns where most of them were built. His clinker brick cottage telephone switching stations "in English Domestic Style," show a fine sense of proportion, excellent Edwardian brickwork, and limited use of polychromy.[11] Rule's English training had made him familiar with Picturesque ideas of composition and siting which were employed to make these equipment warehouses acceptable as mock-domestic buildings on various Alberta main streets. One of Rule's more

Formerly the Red Indian Service Station, this building boasted a sign tower with a stepped back, almost ziggurat form.

The town of Raymond's indoor arena and its neighbour, a former service station.

Peter Rule's drawing of a standard clinker brick switching station, circa 1925.

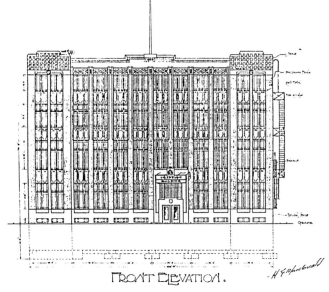

FRONT ELEVATION.

The Alberta Government Telephones Building, Sixth Avenue, Calgary, as shown in Peter Rule's elevation, but not as built. Canadian Architectural Archives, The University of Calgary Library.

elaborate switching stations was designed to minimize objections from the influential residents of Calgary's posh Elbow Park district.

When given the problem of designing AGT's downtown Calgary office and toll building, however, Rule did an abrupt about-face. He applied a severe vertical and rectilinear modern approach to the new four-storey structure. Fireproofing was one of Rule's major concerns in the design of the AGT Building. He also wanted to build a distinguished architectural piece as this was the first major public building to be built in downtown Calgary in nearly a decade. Rule wrote of the Calgary building:

> The design of the building is modern perpendicular style presenting a very strong, substantial and striking appearance. The front elevation is constructed from Don Valley brick and Tyndall stone, while the windows are of steel with cast metal mullions and brests.[12]

The building contained numerous technical innovations for Alberta buildings of the period, including a combination of steel frame with reinforced concrete floors, extensive use of furring and plaster for insulation purposes, service run sub-floors, and the first automatic elevators in Alberta. These innovations served to improve the fireproofing of the building, as well as to demonstrate the association of AGT with the leading edge of the new technologies. While the use of such traditional decorative features as dado, mouldings and marble mosaic on the interiors was accepted practice for similar buildings of the period, the architectural forms of the front elevation certainly were not. Here Rule seems to have combined his knowledge of English brickwork, elements of the Gothic mode of skyscraper design (still the rage in Chicago, New York, and Toronto), and a hint of Modern Movement rectilinearity in glass detailing. The result is one of the most distinguished, if eclectic, early Modern elevations in the province.

The building as it was built.
Alberta Government Telephones.

Rule seems to have gone to great lengths to increase the perceived verticality of this four-storey structure, originally designed for six but never completed to that height. The brick piers are purely decorative and taper as they rise in Gothic fashion with sculpted stone blocks at the top forming medievalized capitals. The Gothic tradition in skyscraper design grew out of nineteenth-century idealization of the Gothic as the most structurally rational and "modern" of the historical styles. Evidence of this preoccupation can be found in John Ruskin's *The Seven Lamps of Architecture* (1849),[13] Pugin's *The True Principles of Pointed or*

Christian Architecture (1840),[14] and Viollet-le-Duc's Entretien sur l'architecture (1872).[15] These writings helped spark the Gothic Revival in Great Britain and the British Empire, notably at Toronto and Calcutta, the two primary repositories of the style. The verticality of Gothic detailing such as piers, buttresses and ogee arches and windows made a relatively easy transition as decorative elements on early twentieth-century office buildings. The buttresses of Brooklyn Bridge, designed by W.A. Roebling in 1883, the New York Woolworth Building by Cass Gilbert in 1913, and the winning entry by Raymond Hood in the Chicago Tribune Office Tower Competition of 1922, are three influential American examples of the industrial and skyscraper traditions of Neo-Gothic design which Rule drew upon in his Calgary building.

Between the capitals of the engaged pilasters of the Sixth Avenue elevation are triangular Art Deco carved stone panels on horizontal frieze blocks. While Rule undoubtedly indulged in these as his exploration of Art Deco skyscraper ornament, he legitimized them during design discussions with AGT as representations of Alberta's vast forest wealth. Incised provincial crests along with crenellations complete the Gothic allusions of the AGT Building. The modernity of the structure is most apparent in the detailing of the windows and cast metal spandrels (or ''brest plates''). The rectilinear modern pattern of both these details and the windows is a worthy knockdown of Mondrian, MacIntosh, or Rietveld, and was unlike anything else yet constructed in the province.[16] While curtain wall technology for a climate such as Calgary's had not yet evolved to the point of allowing unobstructed panes of glass of this size, Rule's details allow him to complete the vertical Gothic intentions of the rest of the structure, while at the same time demonstrating his awareness of the new glass, steel and planar concrete architecture then evolving in Europe. In buildings such as this, Alberta architecture was beginning to move away from its provincial restrictions, and, for the first time, to join the

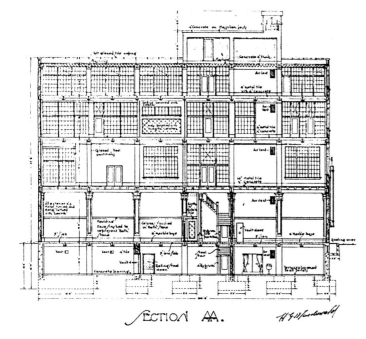

Section of the Alberta Government Telephones Building, Calgary. Canadian Architectural Archives, The University of Calgary Library.

rising tide of internationalism in world architecture.

The motion picture theatre, that quintessential twentieth-century building, was also an early building type through which Modern Movement ideas were spread, safe from the limiting seriousness of grander projects. In Britain, the Odeon chain of cinemas converted so completely to the new modern style in the extensive building programme of the twenties and thirties that the style we now call "Moderne" is referred to even today by the British as the "Odeon Style."

The United States and most of Canada were slower to convert to modernism in cinema design. Here the heyday of gargantuan historicized movie palaces occurred in the 1920s. One of the best Canadian examples of the style was the Spanish village recreated in the interior of the Capitol Theatre in Saskatoon, unfortunately demolished by an Edmonton developer in 1979. The Palace Theatre in Calgary is a more austere, modestly decorated movie palace from the 1920s. When the seating capacities of the Prophetic Bible Institute and Grand Theatre proved inadequate, William Aberhart beamed his influential religio-political broadcasts from the stage of the Palace Theatre for many years.

The conversion to modernism in cinema design in North America was fostered by the Radio City Music Hall. The enormous theatre of the Radio City Music Hall joined the rest of the Rockefeller Center in heavily influencing North American architectural design over the next several decades. The Radio City Music Hall spawned numerous imitators across the continent. Most of them were stripped of the fantastic modernistic decorative programme of the New York building while maintaining its logic of plan and technical innovation. The association of the Rockefeller development with emerging technology was the key to its acceptance and that of other early modern buildings in North America. Rockefeller Center included the headquarters of the Radio Corporation of America (RCA) as well as the

The Capitol Theatre, Saskatoon. Saskatoon Public Library.

The Capitol Theatre's more modest movie palace cousin, the Palace Theatre, Calgary. H. Pollard Collection, Provincial Archives of Alberta.

radio and early television studios of the National Broadcasting Corporation (NBC) and heralded the new age of technological wonder in its sculpture and murals.

Peter Rule weathered the bulk of the Depression in the security of his job as AGT architect. As soon as the Alberta economy made an upturn towards the end of the decade, Rule retired from AGT's employ to oversee the newly established architectural practice of his two sons, John and Peter, and one of their classmates, Gordon Wynn. This company would help to establish Modern architecture firmly in Alberta.

Alberta Government Telephones switching station, downtown Edmonton, circa 1946. Provincial Archives of Alberta.

Rockefeller Center, New York City, designed between 1927 and 1933.

John and Peter Rule and Gordon Wynn were graduates of the short-lived architecture programme at the University of Alberta. They came together to practice in 1938 when they had trouble obtaining work from Edmonton architects still reeling from the effects of the Depression. According to Wynn, things were so tough for Edmonton architects who persevered through the 1930s that "every one of them had his feet up on empty drafting boards, reading the newspaper."[17] With almost nothing better to do, the three young graduates set up their own firm under the watchful eye of the elder Rule.

The University of Alberta architecture programme, where Rule's two boys met Gordon Wynn, was the creation of the *eminence grise* of Alberta architecture throughout the 1920s and 1930s, Cecil Burgess. Burgess came to Alberta as a result of his rendering abilities and a chance meeting with a prominent Canadian architect, Percy Nobbs. A Scottish architect transplanted to Montreal where he taught at McGill, Nobbs met the young Burgess when both were on sketching tours in Italy. Burgess's sketch of the Tower of the Municipio in Verona so impressed Nobbs that he asked the young architect to join his firm as a draftsman. Burgess followed Nobbs from Scotland to Montreal and then to Edmonton, where Nobbs designed the campus plan and early buildings of the University of Alberta. Impressed with his work with Nobbs, the university invited Burgess to stay on as campus architect, with a vague promise of a teaching position at the long-rumoured architecture school. Burgess completed Nobbs's designs for the Arts and Medical Buildings, even now among the most pleasing structures on an architecturally diverse campus.

The University of Alberta Architecture School, after a false start before World War I, was established in the 1920s with Burgess as its head and only full-time staff member. The architecture programme staggered along with a handful of students until the late thirties when it was a victim of budget cuts. So dedicated a teacher was Burgess that he stayed on for a full year past mandatory retirement to see the last class through to graduation, earning wages only the equivalent to their fees, $450.[18] There would not be another architect graduated from an Alberta university architecture school until 1975, when the first students completed their education at the Faculty of Environmental Design, established at the University of Calgary in 1971. Even today, this school produces only 10 percent of the architects Alberta needs each year, and the majority of Alberta architects have come from elsewhere.

The size of the University of Alberta's architecture

Cecil Burgess on one of many sketching tours of Europe. University of Alberta Archives, courtesy of Mrs. C.K. Huckvale.

programme was no indication of the quality of graduate it produced. Among its alumni can be counted such prominent Alberta architects as John Stevenson, L.G. MacDonald, R.M. Stanley, Jack Cawston, and George Lord, as well as Rule, Wynn and Rule. All of these graduates championed Modern architecture, which was surprising considering the traditional English variant of the French Beaux-Arts teaching methods employed by Burgess, and Edmonton's scarcity of Modern buildings. Burgess was to the end extremely skeptical of the value of Modern architecture; he ran the school like an office and put strong emphasis on construction, history, and rendering. It is less surprising in a province that produced Nelly McClung and Emily Murphy that half of the graduating architecture class of 1939 were women, who went on to many years of successful practice in a profession which even today is male-dominated.

Burgess was for many years a member, then chairman, of Edmonton's Town Planning Board, and the extensive boulevards, traffic circles and civic centre enjoyed by Edmontonians are, in part, the products of Burgess's forethought.[19] Burgess, in elegant if somewhat windy Victorian prose, established himself as Alberta's first and foremost architectural historian and critic. He was a tireless crusader for the cause of architecture in Alberta, lecturing frequently to community groups, and contributing criticism and professional news to the RAIC *Journal*. Tireless is also the only word to describe a man who, at the age of seventy, established his own architectural practice, then continued it until his retirement twenty-one years later. Burgess died at the age of 101 in 1971.

The early practice of Rule Wynn and Rule consisted almost entirely of the design of modernistic cinemas for central and northern Alberta towns. Prime among them was the Varscona Theatre, located on the newly developed 109 Street in Edmonton. The Varscona Theatre is one of the best examples of Moderne architecture in Canada. In contrast to its prominence in

The interior of the Varscona Theatre, one of the best examples of Moderne architecture in Canada.
Provincial Archives of Alberta.

the United States, Moderne architecture was not widely built in Canada in the period between 1930 to 1945. Alberta, however, has some of the best examples of the white stucco, streamlined style.[20]

The Varscona Theatre, 109 Street, Edmonton, by Rule Wynn and Rule, 1940. Provincial Archives of Alberta.

As often happens in architectural history, the strength and originality of the design of the Varscona Theatre grew out of a sense of architectural competition with another building. In 1938, Famous Players announced the construction of the Garneau Theatre, a cinema "in the modern style" a few blocks away along 109 Street. It was to be a large theatre by local standards, with nearly eight hundred seats, and no expense was to be spared in its exterior cladding or interior appointments. In 1939, the theatre manager acquired the furniture used by the Royal party during the Edmonton phase of the Royal Tour for use in the lobby. The Edmonton-based Suburban Theatres gave Rule Wynn and Rule the formidable task of "scooping" both the opening date and the modernistic design of the Garneau Theatre, then well under construction. They accomplished both.

The Garneau Theatre, Edmonton, by R. Blakey, with additions attributed to Rule Wynn and Rule. Provincial Archives of Alberta.

The interior of the Garneau Theatre. No expense was spared on the eight-hundred seat theatre. Provincial Archives of Alberta.

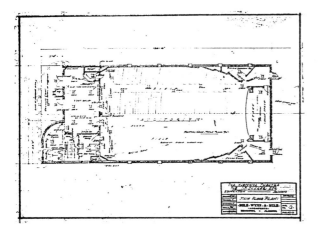

Main floor plan, Varscona Theatre. Canadian Architectural Archives, The University of Calgary Library.

All three members of the firm were soon called off to war, and Peter Rule senior minded the architectural shop through the period of the Varscona Theatre's final design and construction. While John Rule initiated the design before he left, his father was largely responsible for the final design, and for supervision during construction. The design of the Varscona Theatre exhibits the exposure Peter Rule senior must have had to the British Odeon Style during occasional trips to England.

In July 1940, *The Edmonton Bulletin* reported on the opening:

> Designed in streamlined style by Rule, Wynn and Rule, Edmonton Architects, the new theatre, which is of completely fireproof construction with modern air conditioning plant, is a striking land mark in the neighbourhood. Its graceful pilasters and vertical pillars, its noble cornice, curved walls and stately marquee present a striking appearance and command instant attention to the building's

beauty of line and form. These pilasters and pillars contribute to the interest of the building through the light and shade effects they carry. The structure is finished in a gleaming white with a black trim, while windows and doors are finished in an Indian red and black trim.[21]

Unfortunately, the present owner has chosen to cover the "gleaming white and Indian red" with an unauthentic dark green. It is interesting that while the newspaper account comes up with the word "stream-lined," the reporter had to use traditional architectural terminology like "pilaster" and "cornice" in order to describe the roof fins on this anything-but-classical building. This is a recurring problem in architecture: verbal phrases to describe the new visual and spatial developments are slow to form, and a period of confusion inevitably results when the terms of the eclipsed style are used to describe the new one.

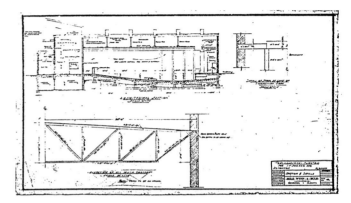

Longitudinal section and related details, Varscona Theatre. Canadian Architectural Archives, The University of Calgary Library.

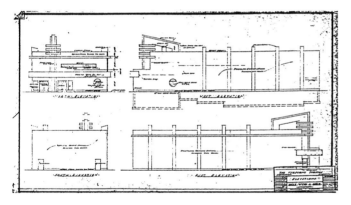

Elevations of the Varscona Theatre, by Rule Wynn and Rule. Canadian Architectural Archives, The University of Calgary Library.

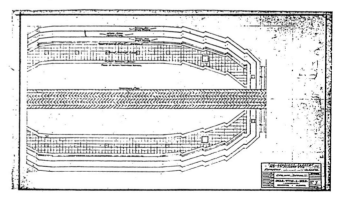

Ceiling detail, Varscona Theatre. Canadian Architectural Archives, The University of Calgary Library.

The Varscona Theatre is remarkable because it anticipates later practice in Modern architecture. The clearly expressed steel structural system on the outside of the building did not become accepted practice for nearly a decade. The parabolic theatre plan and decorative use of acoustic ceiling tile were also ahead

Air conditioning intake at the Varscona Theatre, showing the decorative fins. Provincial Archives of Alberta.

of their time. The building boasts inset glass block windows, and the building's mechanical allusions are reinforced by round nautical windows reminiscent of the battleship-like Coca-Cola Bottling Plant in Los Angeles by R. Derrah (1936).[22] Most remarkable of all is the multi-finned air conditioning intake tower that caps the Varscona Theatre. Beneath the decorative, radiator-like fins is the location of the actual fresh air intake where air is admitted "above the dirt and grime of the street." In the original architect's rendering the intake was even larger and more evident than it now appears.[23]

This same expression, or celebration, of the structural and mechanical guts of a modern building leads, when taken to the limit, to buildings such as Piano and Rodgers's 1977 Georges Pompidou National Art and Cultural Centre in Paris. The Varscona Theatre is a spiritual cousin of the Pompidou Centre in that it also involves the exaggerated expression of building systems and not merely a visual mechanical metaphor, as in the Derrah building and other contemporary Moderne buildings.

Detail of the mechano-like structure of the Georges Pompidou National Art and Cultural Centre, Paris.

Georges Pompidou National Art and Cultural Centre, Paris, by Piano and Rogers.

The celebration of the structural and mechanical guts of a modern building, seen here in the Georges Pompidou National Art and Cultural Centre, Paris.

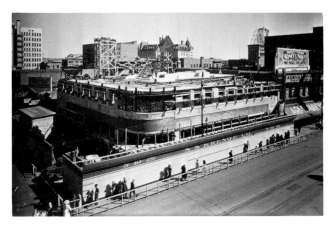

The end of the 1930s brought a renewal of prosperity, especially in northern Alberta. The S.S. Kresge Company store, shown here under construction, was designed by Northwood and Chivers in 1937. The building was demolished in 1980. Glenbow-Alberta Institute, Calgary.

The T. Eaton Company store, Edmonton, also designed by Northwood and Chivers, featured Manitoba Tyndall stone, black granite and custom nickle-plated fixtures.

Alberta's economy began to revive towards the end of the grim thirties and one of the many episodic building booms in the province's history ensued. This one was unusually short-lived, terminated by the outbreak of World War II in 1939. The first expression of this mini-building boom was cinemas, which knew longer and longer lineups through the misery of the Depression. Soon after, downtown Edmonton retailers engaged in a competitive building spree such as Calgary had known in the 1920s. First was the S.S. Kresge Company store on 101 Street, designed by the prominent Winnipeg early modernist firm of Northwood and Chivers in 1937. Soon after, Northwood and Chivers designed a rival structure for the T. Eaton Company, a noble building of Manitoba Tyndall stone and black granite with custom nickle-plated fixtures. The streamlined corners of the building and the contrast of the two stone claddings make this the most prominent building from the 1930s in downtown Edmonton. Moody and Moore, also Winnipeg architects, employed similar cladding materials for their rival store for the Hudson's Bay Company on Jasper Avenue. Their design was somewhat more conservative than that of Northwood and Chivers, but the building is remarkable for the sculpted relief murals on its exterior depicting the company's history, virtually the only extant Alberta examples of the social realist art prevalent during the Depression. Both the T. Eaton Company and The Hudson's Bay Company buildings were published in a retrospective on Canadian architecture in the English magazine *The Architectural Review* in 1942, the only Alberta buildings to be so honoured.

The thirties and forties saw Modern architecture, or a localized, ''modernistic'' variant of it, established in Alberta in the new building types of the cinema, the telephone building, the service station, and the department store. The decade of rapid growth that followed saw the design ideas implicit in Modern architecture spread to virtually every element of the built environment, and throughout Alberta. The rise of

Modern architecture closely tracks the Alberta economy's diversification from a primarily agricultural emphasis to oil and petrochemical production and international prominence in energy finance, research and exploration.

An editorial page from the *Edmonton Bulletin*, New Year's Eve 1938, boasts of the new streamlined buildings constructed recently in the Alberta capital in 1937. Courtesy of City of Edmonton Archives.

The Barron Building, Calgary, designed by Jack Cawston in 1951, as it appears today.

MODERN ARCHITECTURE IN ALBERTA

Calgary entered three decades of tepid economic performance following the collapse of the land boom that preceded World War I. On the other hand, Edmonton, the seat of the provincial government and the University of Alberta, with fledgling manufacturing and processing industries, fared better through this bleak period. With the discovery of a major oil field at Leduc in 1947, provincial and even national economic and urban development patterns were drastically altered. After the early Waterton and Turner Valley oil finds, western Canadian oil industry offices had been located in various portions of Calgary, but when Leduc Imperial Number One came in, a great deal of uncertainty was created in that city. Not only was office space in short supply in Calgary, but Edmonton officials, keen to attract business to their city, were pointing out to oil company executives the advantages of locating their offices closer to the new fields and planned refineries.

Calgary lawyer and theatre owner J.B. Barron sensed a perfect opportunity for the bold mixed-use office tower and cinema complex he long had wanted to build. While Calgary newspapers boasted the announcement of a new office tower almost every week during 1948, by 1949 none had been built or even started. It is to Barron's credit as a developer that he was able to

Cawston's rendering of The Barron Building, Calgary. Courtesy of the Barron Family.

Lars Willumsen of Larwill Construction Ltd. (left) was
general contractor for The Barron Building; J.B. Barron
is seen centre, with Jack Cawston (right).
Courtesy of the Barron Family.

convince as conservative a firm as Great West Life
Assurance Company to grant a mortgage of $850,000[1]
on a stylistically unusual design by Calgary architect
Jack Cawston. Despite technical problems and the lack
of a major tenant, construction started late in 1949, a
particularly bold move given the then tenuous state of
the oil industry in western Canada, and, hence, the
uncertainty of the continuing presence of the industry's
largely American upper management. One waggish
comment of the period had it that the Alberta oil
industry's entire brains and brawn could easily pack up
and leave on one turbo-prop airliner to Dallas! Indeed,
it was not until the mid-1970s, following oil price
increases and evidence of growing Canadian
nationalism, that major oil companies gave up renting
office space, and instead invested in new buildings to
house permanent Canadian headquarters. It is
questionable whether any other major Canadian
industry has ever taken so long to make a physical
commitment to its headquarters city.

The Barron Building opened in May 1951, and not only
played a crucial role in the development of Calgary's
oil patch, but also helped in structuring the city's urban
form. The original tenants included the Sun Oil
Company, the Shell Oil Company, and the Socony
Mobil Oil Company, representing a good proportion of
Calgary's major oil businesses. Ironically, the location of
Barron's building, to the west of downtown Calgary
where the major oil companies remain today, may have
done more to preserve Calgary's architectural heritage
than years of effort by planners and politicians. The
focus of new development in west downtown Calgary
took pressure off the old core in the east end, at the
time a tempting target for obliteration in the form of
"urban renewal." A number of smaller, less imaginative
office buildings were built near the Barron Building to
house oil exploration, consulting, and other petroleum
industry offices. From the vantage point of the
Wrightian penthouse at the top of this building, Jack
Barron watched the rise and fall of oil barons and the

phenomenal growth of this section of Calgary. Without doubt, Barron's bold tower played a catalytic role in keeping oil company headquarters in Calgary, and in steering development to the west side of that city.

The Barron Building shows the competing strains of Modern architecture in Alberta building after World War II. With surprising success, the building combines the massing and modernistic ornament of the New York Art Deco skyscraper, ribbon windows lifted from the International Style, and a Wrightian penthouse. The building combines a cinema with main floor shops and eight storeys of offices topped with a penthouse. It is clad in yellow brick, Tyndall limestone and ornamental aluminum. These last two feature angled chevron and scalloped Art Deco decoration. The stepped back or "wedding cake" massing of the building also refers to the New York Art Deco high-rise. To add yet another ingredient to this stylistic stew, the lobby and interior of the theatre bear a strong resemblance to the late Moderne hotel interiors of Morris Lapidus in Miami Beach.

This type of confusion, even competition, of styles, is characteristic of Canadian architecture as a whole during the period just after World War II. A stripped-down modern classicism reigned in Toronto, with Mathers and Haldenby's 1953 Bank of Nova Scotia office building on King Street West being one of the best examples of this rigid, not really Modern architectural style.[2] The early collaborations of John B. Parkin and John C. Parkin pointed to a distinctly Canadian reworking of the International Style, but their buildings had not received widespread recognition at this point. Page and Steel in Toronto and Thompson, Berwick, Pratt in Vancouver were two major practices deeply committed to Modern architecture. Their work also displays the various design streams at work during the period, including Corbusian, Miesian and Wrightian idioms of the International Style. The B.C. Electric Building (1958), designed by Thompson, Berwick, Pratt,

The Brown Building, Calgary, commissioned by Home Oil Company executive Bob Brown in 1953. The building, designed by Jack Cawston, was completed in 1955; it was demolished in 1981.

with Ron Thom as principal designer, is equal parts Wright, Gropius and Pierluigi Nervi in inspiration. In Quebec, the Beaux-Arts tradition remained strong, not surprisingly, given the cultural links that still exist between Quebec and France. Some Quebec architects such as Parizeau and Blatter did work with Modern, principally Corbusian, ideas.

The various stylistic trends at work in Jack Cawston's Calgary building make more sense given this Canadian context. As Cawston's career progressed, he opted for a purer strain of International Style modern architecture. Impressed with the Barron Building, in 1953 Home Oil Company impressario Bob Brown commissioned Cawston to design a nine-storey office tower on Sixth Avenue. Completed in 1955, but demolished at the height of a more recent boom, the Brown Building was one of Alberta's best examples of high International Style office architecture. This building exhibited the cleanness and clarity of intent and execution which marks the best of this style.

At the same time, Brown indulged Cawston's choice of rich cladding materials. All too often Alberta architects and developers ignored the exhortations of Mies van der Rohe by covering their buildings with the cheapest and shoddiest of materials. The Brown Building was clad in Manitoba Tyndall stone, with crisply detailed blocked window surrounds in the same material. This light grey, easily worked stone was highlighted by bands of red granite, and the first two storeys on the Sixth Avenue elevation were covered in the same material to temper at pedestrian level the building's undeniable austerity. Essentially planar surfaces were highlighted by the shadows cast by the banding and window surrounds. The off-centre composition of the entrance and of the banded corner windows showed a respect by the architect for streetscape that is not evident a few years later with the rise of the carte blanche empty plaza, such as those encouraged by Calgary's Plus 15 Bonus System of the 1970s.[3] When the building was demolished, one element was preserved;

Brown's lavishly finished boardroom was moved to another tower, a last vestige of his collaboration with Cawston. Like many of Alberta's best designers, Cawston quickly fell from favour and died a sadly early death.

In 1955, the long-promised Federal Building finally opened in Edmonton, having been delayed by changes in governments, the war, and other building priorities. The office building had been designed during the Depression as a make-work project and had been only slightly updated. The architect was G.H. MacDonald, who began his career as a draftsman in Nova Scotia, studied architecture at McGill University, and then entered practice with H.A. Magoon in Edmonton in 1911. The rather tired and instantly dated Edmonton Federal Building was the last major project of his long and prolific career. A further illustration of government conservatism in design, federal officials apparently thought that money would be saved by using plans nearly twenty years old from an architect on the verge of retirement. The inset marble and nickle-plated metal work of the lobby create one of the liveliest Art Deco interiors remaining in Alberta, even though this is an interior of the 1930s built in the 1950s. It is also one of the last Art Deco interiors built anywhere, thanks to the long delay in construction.

During the 1950s, both the economy and the architecture of Alberta took the directions that would culminate in the boom of the late seventies. The early fifties saw mounting waves of resource-generated growth sweep the province. Perhaps unavoidably, an increase in architectural quality did not accompany the increase in the number of buildings constructed, as illustrated by the bluntly ugly Petroleum Building in Calgary, a homely and expedient structure designed by Rule Wynn and Rule. After 1955, Calgary and Edmonton, excepting only tiny clusters of Victoriana, entirely rebuilt their downtown areas. This was an opportunity for innovation and public amenity which few cities anywhere have encountered on such a scale. The architectural history

The Edmonton Federal Building, designed by G.H. MacDonald, was completed in 1955.

Inset marble and nickle-plated metal work in the Federal Building, Edmonton, created one of the liveliest Art Deco interiors extant.

of the past three decades in Alberta is in general a catalogue of missed possibilities. The "get-it-out-by-Friday" attitude that a boom inevitably generates often has tragic implications for architectural design. The scale and strength of the post-World War II boom, allied with large-scale private and public development, militated against an original, carefully considered, communicative architecture. Architects are not tested to the limits of their abilities when their buildings are completely leased even before construction commences, as was the case in Calgary for most of the 1970s. In addition, the reigning design ideology promoted a bland generic internationalism, and the adapted particularities of regionalism were anathema.

Meticulous and appropriate detailing is needed particularly for the visual success of Modern architecture, but the boom mentality of Alberta, coupled with a lack of a secondary building products industry, meant that this crucial phase of the design process all too often was glossed over. Mies van der Rohe often would spend weeks on a corner detail of I-beams on a building such as the Seagram Tower, or he would build elaborate models and photographic simulations to study window proportions. In the rush of development, neither Alberta architects, their clients, nor the public had patience for such esoteric concerns. The cheapest of cladding materials, assembled quickly into a derivative design, became the hallmark of Alberta design.

An exception to this trend was the triple tower and podium development erected in Calgary by the Irish Guinness brewing interests in the early 1960s. While present tastes might question the lurid green fibreglass spandrel panels on the towers, the architects, including Rule Wynn and Rule, carefully detailed the elevations, interiors, and massings in one complete conception. The design motif of the hexagon is featured on the spandrel panels, on pedestrian canopies, lobby walls, and even light diffuser boxes. This cladding colour and the mosaic harps and angels are allusions, unusually

The Petroleum Building, Calgary, by Rule Wynn and Rule, 1951. H. Pollard Collection, Provincial Archives of Alberta.

explicit for a high Modern building, to the Irish source of the Guinness fortune.

A cladding material similar to that of the Guinness towers was used to decorate the elevation of Edmonton's old City Hall in cream and chocolate brown checkerboard fashion. Having recently completed a new City Hall, the city fathers decided that the 1913 brick and sandstone structure did not present a sufficiently progressive architectural image for the booming "Oil Capital of Canada." Taking action that would make the European fathers of the Modern Movement wince, they installed a decorative glass curtain wall in the late 1950s to re-face the building. It still stands on Churchill Square, having served as the city's police headquarters for several decades. The fathers of the Modern Movement had first put forward their architectural ideas as an end to styles, the supercession of petty historical symbolism by a triumphant rationalism. As this example demonstrates, their ideas had evolved into what can only be called a highly symbolic style, as thin and transparent as a pane of glass.

Architect Kelvin Stanley designed Edmonton's prestigious new City Hall in a version of the International Style that refers to many periods and elements of buildings in the career of Le Corbusier. One of the first major downtown projects in Edmonton after World War II, the City Hall and its controversial "spaghetti tree" fountain captured the imagination of the bustling city as few buildings have before or since. Mayor William Hawrelak and the council intended it to be an unabashed symbol of modernism and progress, and the building accomplished this well. The Edmonton City Hall contains a virtual glossary of design principles of the Corbusian International Style. There is an emphasis on horizontality and volumetric manipulation put together in an off-centre composition. Such elements of the Le Corbusier version of the style as ribbon windows, solar fins, a sculptural penthouse, and pilotis are in evidence. Massing of the Edmonton City

Elveden House, part of the Guinness Complex, Calgary, 1961. Provincial Archives of Alberta.

Hall is vaguely reminiscent of Le Corbusier's Pavillon Suisse at Paris's Cité Universitaire. Modern architecture, because of its choice of unadorned planar surfaces, depends on a richness of material surface to achieve any degree of sensuousness. The veined black marble elevator lobbies and green slate floors of the building make such an impact.

Le Pavillon Suisse, Cité Universitaire, Paris, by Le Corbusier, 1930-32. Collection, The Museum of Modern Art, New York.

The Edmonton City Hall, by Dewar, Stevenson, Stanley and Seton, 1957.

By the end of the 1950s, the most eye-catching architectural developments were not occurring downtown in "high style" buildings, but at the ill-defined edge of town. The late 1950s and the 1960s are noteworthy for the rise of a pervasive and symbolically rich vernacular architecture, that of the automobile-oriented commercial strip. By the mid-1960s Calgary had the largest non-military colony of Americans in the world, numbering fifty thousand. Along with the influx of oil men came the franchise entrepreneur and the architecture of muffler shops, used car lots, and hamburger chains. This huge foreign presence had an undeniable economic and architectural influence. In particular, the fast-growing Macleod Trail area of Calgary took on the appearance of the generalized American Strip that is the same from Mississauga to Mississippi.[4] Macleod Trail boasts some of the best, or at least some of the most extreme, Canadian examples of this new vernacular architecture.

By the 1970s, strip architecture had come to haunt architectural theorists concerned with the limited cultural impact of the bleak abstractions of the International Style. In 1932, architect John Lyle, seeing the emergence of the Modern Movement, had predicted the waning of public interest in architecture if it eliminated "symbolism in the form of fresh, bold, contemporary decoration."[5] The simultaneous death of public interest in "high" architecture and the rise of a commercially successful brash strip architecture may have proven Lyle's prediction correct.

Taking a cue from Marshall McLuhan's studies of mass media and pop culture,[6] the American architect and critic Robert Venturi led one of the first and most important appreciative forays into the strip and its architecture in his seminal book, *Learning From Las Vegas: The Forgotten Symbolism of Architectural Form.*[7] Venturi and his colleagues identified two typologies of strip architectural form, the "Duck" and the "Decorated Shed." The Duck is a building whose very form becomes a symbol, like the hamburger stand in

An example of the symbolically-rich architecture of the automobile-oriented Macleod Trail, Calgary.

Welcome to Canada, land of the thirty-foot Mountie! This example of strip architecture can be seen in the main street of Cardston, Alberta. Provincial Archives of Alberta.

Overscale hood ornament or Neo-Ski-Jump? This car showroom was designed by W. Milne.

the shape of a hamburger, or the unvarnished Modernist strain of programmatic expressionism. The Decorated Shed involves the application of decoration or large-scale signage to a simple structure. Macleod Trail has its share of both Ducks and Decorated Sheds, with the overall symbolism showing a propensity towards space exploration and a borrowed history. The architectural symbolism of Macleod Trail exhibits tension between an imagined technological future of sputniks, rocket-ships, and robot car-washes, and an equally fantastic manufactured past of mansard roofs, coach lamps, and fiberglass log shacks.

The symbolically rich formfulness and the brash and fearless plundering of architectural history that one sees along the Macleod Trail form a neat counterpoint to the austere developments in "high" architecture of the period. The arid, abstract, rectilinear steel, glass and concrete architecture spawned by the Modern Movement was so pervasive in post-war building that it fulfilled the prophecy implicit in the Hitchcock-Johnson term, the International Style, by being constructed with little variation around the world. Corporations wanted architectural packaging as slick as cellophane, and architects gladly provided it. Never before or since has there been such a coincidence of marketplace minimalism with High Art packaging.

A comparison between the Flamingo Motel, by A. Dale, with the Milner Building, by Rule Wynn and Rule, reveals the contrast between high and low-style buildings designed by architects. The thirty-foot pink flamingo and the neon-covered futuristic concrete pylon of the motel take to the stream of Macleod Trail traffic like a duck to water. The Milner Building, on the other hand, is a rather timid and tentative investigation of the International Style in Edmonton's first major post-war high-rise office tower. The mullions and spandrels of the tower lack the articulation and finish needed to make a Miesian curtain wall façade read well.[8] The building also contains references to Le Corbusier in the massing

The Flamingo Motel, Macleod Trail, Calgary.

The Milner Building, Edmonton, by Rule Wynn and Rule, 1958, was a tentative investigation of the International Style. Provincial Archives of Alberta.

of the podium, reminiscent of his original design for the United Nations Secretariat in New York, and the mildly developed piloti system, akin to the Unité d'Habitation in Marseilles, but neither is pushed far enough to read as such. The Milner Building was perhaps most remarkable for its lobby mural which portrays the western boom from frontier fort to jetliner,

This mural, portraying the western boom from frontier fort to jetliner, was designed for the lobby of the Milner Building. It is now installed at a gas company's remote office. Provincial Archives of Alberta.

Bow Valley Square, Calgary, designed by Webb Zerafa Menkes Housden, Toronto, 1972-81.

now banished to a remote gas company building. Somehow the pop extravaganza of a building such as the Flamingo Motel reveals more of the sensibility of the period than does the valueless grid of the Milner Building.

The most disturbing trend throughout this latter period of Alberta architecture is that the sources of design are almost exclusively European and American for both vernacular and high architecture. Edmonton-born Marshall McLuhan warned that the rise of mass culture and the media, which sells its goods and values, have forged a new global community in which traditional national and regional cultures lose most of their meaning and importance.[9] While even McLuhan later retreated from this extreme stand, this shift from local, regional, and national towards the international is evident in the design and architecture of this period. Architectural plans for chain restaurants in Alberta generally come off the shelves of California fast-food design specialists.[10] Only the awkward double doors are an accommodation to our climate.

Just as surely, high architecture was in the thrall of the idea of Total Design that grew out of the Bauhaus and the Modern Movement in European architecture, or its variant transplanted into the fertile soil of post-war North American architecture schools. The international architectural magazines have become increasingly important, and the time-lag between the construction of an innovative building, its appearance in journals, and the design of an imitation in Alberta has become shorter and shorter through the modern era. This rapid compression of time and place makes an architecture of specificity and considered locality nearly impossible.

With the rise of corporate International Style architecture came the increasing importance of Toronto and New York architects to major projects in Edmonton, and more particularly, Calgary. Major corporations tend to pick architects from the city in which their head offices are located, meaning that a branch plant economy leads to branch plant architecture. Cadillac and Porsche architecture is not normally found in Alberta; sturdy Buicks and Oldsmobiles of middle management are the rule. This generalization is not absolutely true, for the Alberta work of one major Toronto firm, Webb Zerafa Menkes Housden, is among the best of modern high-rise design in Canada. The huge multi-phased Bow Valley Square by this firm has a deeply modelled brilliant white pre-cast concrete elevation which carefully catches and modulates the late afternoon orange Calgary sunlight.

Along Second Street SW from Bow Valley Square is Canada Place, designed by Boris Zerafa, a brick-clad tower that housed the first head offices of Petro-Canada. The bevelled plan and massing of Canada Place show some of the sculptural and colour potential of the later Modern office tower. These design features were used by the architect to compensate for a site constrained by adjacent buildings. The unusual shape, colour, and especially the Crown-owned occupant, led the Calgary oil patch to nickname this building "Red Square," a moniker flaunted in the 1984 new headquarters for Petro-Canada, designed by Webb Zerafa Menkes Housden, where red granite was employed.

In a near fatal reduction of the architectural problem to its skeletal basics, Modern architecture had also in many ways neatly eliminated much of the traditional role of the architect as designer. Under the influence of the Modern Movement, architects dreamed of massive megastructures[11] and societal reform through Total Design, while at the same time engineers and contracting firms were getting more efficient and, in many ways, more artful at designing Modern buildings than were registered architects. Architects are now often reduced to the tokenism of floor plan fine-tuning or finish and colour selections and signage, especially within the tight design and economic constraints of the speculative office tower. Today, less than half of all new Alberta buildings are designed by registered architects,

The brick-clad Canada Place by Webb Zerafa Menkes Housden, Calgary, 1976.

Mies van der Rohe's astoundingly prescient 1922 scheme for a concrete office block. Photograph courtesy of Mies van der Rohe Archive, The Museum of Modern Art, New York.

a trend readily discernible in the rest of North America. The rise to prominence in Alberta of five or six corporate architecture firms which employ engineers, interior designers, planners, construction managers, and many other technical specialists, is symptomatic of this trend. This handful of firms built the majority of Alberta public buildings during the 1960s and 1970s and did so with such efficiency and such mastery of stripped-down, bare-bones design that there was real worry for a period about the survival of smaller firms.

The pre-cast concrete buildings of a design-and-build firm, such as Batoni-Bowlen, outshine many comparable towers designed by architects. Attacked by developers who control key portions of the development process on the one hand, and by politically powerful engineers on the other, Alberta architects have had plenty of reasons for self-doubt. After all, the argument goes, if a simplistic rectilinear aesthetic rules, then any engineer with a T-square and a decent sense of proportion can usurp much of an architect's traditional preserve, while offering the added benefit of a more systematic technical background.

The pre-cast concrete Nelco Building, Calgary, designed by Hasegawa Engineering.

Modern architecture reaches the vanishing point: mirrored towers in Calgary.

Modern architecture reached the vanishing point in Alberta by the late 1970s, and one might ask whether the only difference between architects and engineers is taste in waiting room graphics. The mirrored elevations of Alberta office towers of the late 1970s take the puritanical direction of too much of Modern architecture to its logical conclusion. These buildings, in reflecting uncritically the environment around them, have neatly eliminated nearly all issues for the architecture of the façade. Gone are considerations of the size and proportion of window openings, and the modelling of the façade. The planar, mirrored, building eliminates consideration of colour, texture, finish, even shape and mass. The forest of speculative high-rise office towers that grew during the sixties and seventies gives mute witness to these economic and cultural trends. However, this forest saw the emergence of some young and fiercely original architects in the late 1960s: furry mammals to question and taunt the dinosaur of Modern architecture.

Model for the Western Provinces Pavilion at Expo '67, by Beatson Stevens. Provincial Archives of Alberta .

International architecture with Canadian overtones, or Canadian architecture with international aspects? The Edmonton International Airport by the Parkin Partnership. Provincial Archives of Alberta.

TOWARDS AN ALBERTA ARCHITECTURE

While the corporate International Style came to dominate Alberta architecture in the mid-sixties, the beginnings of an adapted regionalism could also be seen. Culminating in the radical visions of Expo '67 in Montreal, Canadian architecture as a whole was exploring new and more indigenous forms throughout this period. Although the work in this era by Arthur Erickson, Ray Affleck, Moshe Safdie, John Andrews, and the Parkin Partnership is still mainstream Modern architecture, it is at least an identifiably Canadian reworking of such Modern Movements as Brutalism, or the Mies or Neutra-inspired International Style. A number of Alberta buildings from the late 1960s and early 1970s show a growing currency with new ideas in world architecture. These new Alberta buildings, while falling short of a true architectural regionalism, at least offer refreshingly novel approaches to modern architecture, and are less apt crudely to mimic design innovations from elsewhere.

One of the most interesting Alberta buildings from the late sixties is the Calgary Centennial Planetarium by Hugh MacMillan and Jack Long. The building combines the board-formed, rough concrete *béton brut*, with forms that clearly allude to medievál castles, so loved by Le Corbusier.[1] The official stylistic label for the stream of Modern architecture utilizing rough-edged concrete buildings is the poetically apt "Brutalist." The

Calgary Centennial Planetarium has exactly the right element of a science fiction movie set to complement its function as a centre of popular astronomy. It is particularly remarkable for its prominent location in a city well-known for architectural conservatism. While the plan is unworkable in places, and the colour palette monotonous, the building has proved to be remarkably popular, as have most Alberta examples of Late or Post-Modern architecture.

The Calgary Centennial Planetarium, by MacMillan-Long Architects, 1967.

Edmonton architect Don Bittorf designed a superb low-key art gallery that uses Brutalist elements in a surprisingly warm and humane manner. The understatement of the Edmonton Art Gallery is in direct contrast to the braggadocio of the Boston City Hall-inspired looming forms of the Alberta Court House behind it, the two forming a set-piece on Brutalism in architecture. Both the colour and board-forming of the concrete of the art gallery soften this building which might have appeared like a squat bunker had it not been so carefully detailed. The sky-lit great staircase of the gallery is one of the most handsome spaces of any building in the province.

A French immigrant to Alberta, Philippe Delesalle, designed a remarkable building in Banff, the Whyte Museum of the Canadian Rockies, that harkens back to Frank Lloyd Wright's Banff Park Pavilion. The design of this building masters a warm and humane strain of Modern architecture continued by the American architect Louis Kahn and the Finnish architect Alvar Aalto. The massive cast-concrete structure of the building, clearly visible in the library reading room, is reminiscent of the log-truss system used in the Banff Park Pavilion sixty years earlier. The frank expression of the structural truss, which was accomplished in a single two-day pour of concrete, plays against the warm cedar cladding, copper roof, and Rundle stone interior. The Banff building is Late Modern architecture at its most articulate, and warmly resonant with the particularities of place.

Edmonton Art Gallery, by Don Bittorf.

Whyte Museum of the Canadian Rockies, Banff, by Philippe Delesalle.

Alberta's most radical, uneven, but brilliant architect of this period is Douglas Cardinal. Philip Johnson, a founding father of the Modern Movement in North America, has called Douglas Cardinal "one of the few true Post-Modern Architects, one who actually builds, not just talks about it."[2] Recently departing from his Modernist roots to design a series of historicist and decorated projects, Johnson has chosen to apply the label "Post-Modern" to St. Mary's Roman Catholic Church, Red Deer, and the Grande Prairie Regional College, both curving, brick structures designed by Cardinal. These designs attack one of the central canons of Modern architecture, the sanctity of rectilinear geometry. The very mode of Cardinal's attack, in which he replaces an exclusively rectilinear architecture with an exclusively curvilinear one, shows, however, that his roots and sensibilities still lie with the Modern Total Design philosophy. Once an engineer, always an engineer, goes the saying, but its architectural equivalent might be once a modernist, always a modernist. Moreover, Cardinal's architecture resurrects a Modern Movement which had died with the rise of the International Style: Expressionism. The curving, spatial complexity of such 1920s Expressionist buildings as Erich Mendelsohn's Einstein Tower in Potsdam inspired Cardinal's architecture, as did the formal experiments of Eero Saarinen including, for example, Trans World Airlines (TWA) Terminal at Kennedy airport in New York.

The Einstein Tower, Potsdam, Germany, 1920-21, designed by Erich Mendelsohn. Photograph courtesy of The Museum of Modern Art, New York.

Red Deer-born Cardinal, a Métis, went through a period of politicization with native Indian causes. He sees the spiritual regimen of the sweat house as giving the personal strength and inspiration needed to accomplish his highly original architecture. He associates the mechanistic limitations of rectilinear geometry with all the hardness and insensitivity of modern life. Cardinal would be only a minor rebel if he did not also take a unique and sensitive approach to the programming of space needs. He carefully elaborates his radical forms as resonant shells for the complex webs of action, interaction and reflection which constitute the use of a modern institutional building.

The inspiration for Cardinal's radical architecture, however, lies more in the history of his own discipline than in his ethnic background. Cardinal calls his work "Modern Baroque" in contradistinction to the Mannerist trend of such Post-Modern architects as Philip Johnson, Charles Moore, or Michael Graves. Cardinal argues that the end of a classicist tradition in architectural history has led inevitably to either Mannerism or the Baroque, his prime example being the modification of Renaissance architecture into these two traditions. His personal and political sensibilities lead him towards the sensualism of the latter over the intellectualism of the former.

Cardinal's first major building, St. Mary's Church in suburban Red Deer, is also his most successful, and one of Alberta's great architectural treasures. The building arcs up in a great three-dimensional spiral around and away from the altar. Despite its challenging design, the structure is beautifully adapted to the procession and ritual of the Mass. At one and the same time it has an openness and an intimacy, qualities that curiously anticipated the Vatican reforms in Roman Catholic church design guidelines which followed a few years after its construction. The design was technically innovative, employing a unique cable steel web roof which required one of the largest ever computer applications to an Alberta building in order to calculate the stress resolutions. Extraordinarily, the exercise proved unnecessary as Cardinal's preliminary intuitive notions of organic form and structure had been correct.

A building as original and striking as St. Mary's Church is inevitably the product of a liaison of an imaginative architect with a patient and open client. Working for many months with Father Merx and his parishioners in Red Deer, Cardinal produced nearly a dozen studies of St. Mary's Church before the ever-evolving organic forms were "frozen" in their present shapes. Cardinal

St. Mary's Roman Catholic Church arcs up in a great three-dimensional spiral around and away from the altar.

works extensively in study models, but has also developed one of Canada's most advanced architectural computer graphics systems, which he feels will aid in the design of his highly complex buildings. There is something ironic in the sight of this romantic, radical architect assembling the drawings of his swirling buildings on a visual display terminal with a light pen—a little like meeting Henry David Thoreau on a Boeing 747. Cardinal is not the first artist in architecture or any other discipline to use such ironies and disjunctions to fire his creative force. Cardinal's more recent projects are increasingly concerned with energy and local materials, and he may be moving from the purely sculptural approach of his earlier buildings to the beginnings of a truly regional architecture, if a personal and iconoclastic one.

St. Mary's Roman Catholic Church, Red Deer, designed by Douglas Cardinal in 1968.

The sky-lit Tyndall stone altar of St. Mary's Roman Catholic
Church. Courtesy of Douglas Cardinal.

If Cardinal had stopped work after designing St. Mary's
Church he would have been remembered as one of
many Alberta architects who turned a church design
into an exercise in expressionism. He did not stop
there, but followed by adapting his form language to

the infinitely more complex space needs of a Regional College at Grande Prairie (1974), and a Provincial Government Services Centre at Ponoka (1977). While cost limitations resulted in plain, stripped-down interior finishes, Cardinal has taken his sensuous spatial vision to its logical conclusion in these two buildings. He writes of his Grande Prairie building:

> The present rigid systems of design based on a system of aesthetics crystallized, ritualized and enshrined as contemporary architectural taste is insufficient to meet the role of cultural transformation that this education centre must play. The Grande Prairie Regional College involves a new approach to architecture in which the people within the organism itself meet the ever-changing needs and problems and so create the whole fabric.

The Grande Prairie Regional College, designed by Douglas Cardinal in 1974.

Douglas Cardinal adapted his form language to the complex space needs of the Grande Prairie Regional College.

The design cries out for growth, expansion, innovation and change. It breathes freedom. Like a plant it needs only nourishment to thrive and develop. The people in it are that nourishment. The organism itself feathers into the landscape, following the natural contours. The plan does not separate buildings as is found in southern climates, where the warmth makes wide spaces between buildings an asset. In this design for northern climates, not only does the unity of the design give an organic power but it is also more efficient in terms of technology.[3]

The fallacies implicit in this organic, or organismic, view of design are obvious; a building need not take on the very organic forms of its surroundings in order to fit in. Cardinal's curves are as arbitrary and intellectual an intrusion into the natural environment as are the steel and glass forms of his admirer Philip Johnson's famous house in New Canaan, Connecticut.

Douglas Cardinal designed the Ponoka Government Services Centre in 1977.

Cardinal's sensuous spatial vision is taken to its logical conclusion in the Ponoka Government Services Centre.

The stairwell, balconies and atrium of the Ponoka Government Services Centre .
Photograph by Cam Huth.

Cardinal's book, *Of the Spirit: Writings by Douglas Cardinal,* is a polemic like virtually all writings by architects; a pose, a position, a response, usually to previous architectural polemic. That rationalism suffers in this activity is obvious, but so much of what the architect does, and what society demands of him, is not readily made explicit and rational. On closer inspection, the poses Cardinal and Johnson take have much in common. Both are iconoclasts; both push an architecture which communicates by means of powerful forms over subtle modulation; both are inheritors of an American architectural and philosophical tradition begun by Thomas Jefferson, who was as content arguing the rights of individuals as building log cabins

The gyrating, topsy-turvy vision of the theatre of the Grande Prairie Regional College, one of the most stunning interiors in Alberta.

or Olympian campuses. To look out from the Rotunda of the University of Virginia, or Philip Johnson's living room in New Canaan, or the atrium of the Grande Prairie Regional College, is to take part in an architect's arguments about the unity of man and his institutions with nature. The gyrating, topsy-turvy vision of the theatre of the Grande Prairie Regional College is one of the most stunning interiors in the province. While even Cardinal will admit that these buildings do not have the power to inspire and uplift people universally, as the pioneers of the Modern Movement hoped the new architecture would do, they do bring a refreshing playfulness, sensualism, and questioning of conventional wisdom and values to Alberta architecture.

Cardinal's friend, Peter Hemingway, shares his politicization (albeit of a different ideological cant), but Hemingway's designs come closer to the mainstream of Late Modern architecture. Hemingway seems capable of understanding and artfully quoting almost any stream of Late Modern architecture. His building for Stanley Engineering, on Kingsway Avenue in Edmonton, is a clear and eloquent reference to Eero Saarinen's rusting cor-ten steel John Deere Office Building in Moline, Illinois. The detailing on the Massey Medal-winning Stanley Engineering Building and later Hemingway buildings have an almost Japanese quality of quiet refinement. Edmonton's Coronation Swimming Pool from 1968 also won a Massey Medal, and here Hemingway has clearly referred to the National

Peter Hemingway's 1968 design for the Stanley Engineering Building won the Massey Medal, Canada's highest architectural award.

Gymnasium and Pool in Tokyo by Kenzo Tange, a Japanese student of Le Corbusier. Hemingway's geometric romance with the pyramid has been pursued through several fundamentalist churches and the extremely popular Muttart Conservatory in Edmonton. Hemingway's more recent interests have steered away from such formalist concerns and towards more overt historic reference, not always with success.

The association of Toronto architects Barton Myers and Jack Diamond with Edmonton's Richard L. Wilkin resulted in two of the most urbane urban Alberta buildings of the 1970s, the Housing Union Building (HUB) student residence, and the Citadel Theatre, both in Edmonton. The two buildings exhibit a sensitivity to the urban fabric that is a long way from the valueless grids and the "ignore the site" philosophy of the early days of Modern architecture. The HUB residence originally was designed to allow a city street to run underneath thus saving precious land around the University of Alberta campus. This street was blocked off almost immediately after the opening of the building, not the first time that the organizing idea of a project, the *parti* in Beaux-Arts terms, was eliminated without architectural detriment to the building to which it gave shape. The HUB also shows the influence of Italian theorist and architect Aldo Rossi, as demonstrated in his 1968 Gallaratese II Apartment Complex outside Milan. Rossi advocates an architecture shaped fundamentally by the application to generic building types of abstract and bare surfaces. The volumes, but never the surfaces, are distilled from history. Such interior touches as exposed air ducts and interior windows at the HUB provide an industrial aesthetic "kit-of-parts" look borrowed from James Stirling and Charles and Ray Eames, while the austere exterior bears a startling resemblance to Mies van der Rohe's Wiessenhofsiedlung Housing of 1927 in Stuttgart.

The red Medicine Hat brick of the Citadel Theatre was a gentle inflection by the architects towards the brick Alberta Hotel and other turn-of-the-century buildings in

Detail of the Stanley Engineering Building in Edmonton, showing the oxidizing cor-ten steel girders.

An exterior view of the north end of the Housing Union Building, Edmonton.

An interior view of the Housing Union Building showing the windows of student apartments fronting onto the shop-filled galleria.

the Jasper East grouping, an area they felt was important and worth preserving. Like the HUB, the Citadel Theatre was the result of the creative use of design constraints. Edmonton city planners wanted a ground-level pedway through the building, further complicating a site already limited by the structural spans of an underground parking garage. The architects, Myers and Wilkin, actually capitalized on the restrictions, and made the shaped tiers of theatre seats a major sculptural element. They then wrapped the lobby and stairs around them in a glass-sheathed celebration of seeing and being seen at intermissions. Both buildings propose a new urbanism for Alberta: in the HUB, a climate-protected galleria throbbing with street life; and at the Citadel Theatre, a visual projection of the act of theatre, even to animate the entire Churchill Square area.

The interior of The Citadel Theatre. Courtesy of R.L. Wilkin, Architects, Edmonton.

The Citadel Theatre, Edmonton.
Courtesy of The Citadel Theatre, Edmonton.

Alberta architecture comes full circle with a return to Victorian historicism in an intriguing project by former R.L. Wilkin associates David Murray and David Lieberman. Evergreen Memorial Gardens, located northeast of Edmonton, wanted a suitably non-denominational memorial for the graveyard there. The firm had acquired elements of the limestone and brick clock tower of the former Edmonton Post Office designed in 1911 by David Ewart, Dominion Public Works architect but, sadly, demolished. The city had planned to rebuild the highly decorated clock tower in front of the Plaza Hotel, but salvaged elements were misnumbered, costs escalated, and a hulking, rusting steel frame designed by an Edmonton Planning Department employee was erected instead to house the clock works. Murray and Lieberman have taken carved limestone decorative elements salvaged from Ewart's noble tower, combined them with a new cast-concrete frame and dome (complete with occulus), to create a surprisingly noble and wistful monument for Evergreen Memorial Gardens.

Edmonton Post Office, designed by Dominion Public Works architect David Ewart. Glenbow-Alberta Institute, Calgary.

The Funerary Memorial for Evergreen Memorial Gardens.

In all these buildings, an Alberta, prairie, or even distinctively Canadian architectural character is only faintly outlined; a silhouette becoming a sketch, but not yet a rendered drawing. The internationalism of Modern architecture, enforced by business organization, global technologies, and the infusion of a mass-media dominated culture lingers on and an architectural regionalism seems unattainable. Another of Alberta's great building booms is over, and with it the last great chance to mould the province's cities to reflect the current self-perception of its people. An Alberta architecture, should one emerge in the next decade, is likely to remain but a ripple on the expansive grid of Modern architecture in Alberta.

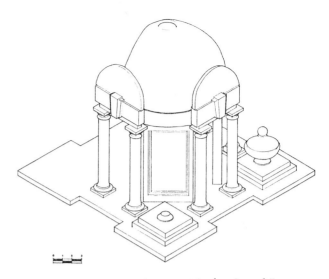

Axonometric drawing of Funerary Memorial for Evergreen Memorial Gardens, near Edmonton, by R.L. Wilkin associates David Murray and David Lieberman, 1977. Courtesy R.L. Wilkin, Architects, Edmonton.

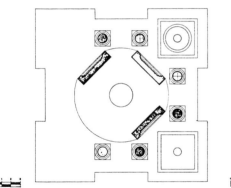

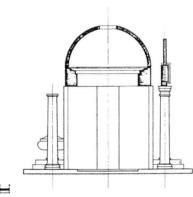

Additional drawings of the Funerary Memorial for Evergreen Memorial Gardens. Courtesy R.L. Wilkin, Architects, Edmonton.

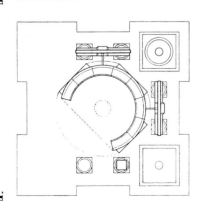

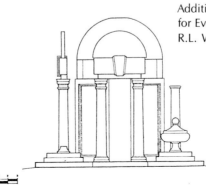

CONCLUSION

During the period in which Modern architecture, and, in particular, the International Style, held sway, most of urban Alberta as we now know it was built. Alberta is marked more by the functionalist forms and philosophies of modernism than any other place in the world. Le Corbusier, who in his last projects questioned many of the tenets of Modern architecture, might be taken aback by the hardness and coldness of an entire city, such as Calgary, built in variants of the International Style. We can assume this would be true by charting the great Swiss architect's reaction to the modern energy of New York City. He admired it from afar, and was still taken by its vibrant charms on his first visit in the early 1930s. But on subsequent trips and upon developing a greater intimacy with the American metropolis, he became aware of the aesthetic, social and cultural implications of the totally modern and mechanized city. The principles of modern urbanism he and the other members of the Conférence Internationale d'Architecture Moderne proposed have proven to be increasingly inappropriate for cities far from the European capitals in which they were conceived.

The Modern Movement was an appropriate response to the situation in European design and architecture earlier in this century. The Modern Movement began, and knew its greatest success, in response to a Europe ravaged by war and weighed down by an oppressive and inescapable weight of history. The connection of the avant-garde, progressive ideals of the Modern Movement with the corporate mode of business and design in North America is one of the stranger and most influential turns of fate in the entire history of architectural ideas. Unavoidably, some of the

movement's principles have little relevance to the far corners of the globe to which they have spread, just as in the last century principles of European classicism looked awkward and difficult in colonial reworkings.

The remaining years of this century will inevitably see a reevaluation of the principles of Modern architecture. A new stylistic revolution, similar to the one which preceded it, may eliminate the best aspects of Modern architecture in a wholesale conversion to a new style. Whether that style will be the bizarre hybrid which is Post-Modernism, the avant-garde revivalism of the Neo-Modern, or some other variant, it is too early to tell. If a widespread popular reaction against Modern architecture occurs in Alberta, as it has in parts of Europe and the United States, even its best elements may be lost: the Modern baby tossed out with the Modern bathwater. The real culprit in the creation of Alberta's heretofore largely mediocre architecture may be the very notion of a single architectural style, especially one accepted unquestioningly from taste-makers elsewhere, then meekly elaborated by a province and a nation too hidebound to define their own architectural culture. Surely there must be a place in an evolving stylistic pluralism for a local or regional style, an Alberta architecture, and, with it, a Canadian architecture?

What will be the direction that Alberta architecture now takes? The pace of the unrelenting two-decade boom of the 1960s and 1970s did not allow architects, developers, planners, or the public time for reflection, let alone debate or criticism. Seldom has a city so wantonly sold off its architectural heritage to the highest bidder as Edmonton did and continues to do.

Edmonton lost most of its Victorian public building legacy during the 1960s and 1970s in a series of trade-offs frequently for mediocre modern development. The Carnegie Library gave way to the Alberta Government Telephones Tower complex, the provincial supreme court to Edmonton Centre, the old post office to the Edmonton Plaza Hotel. Calgary entered the demolition derby as well: in 1979, Calgary built more square footage of new office space than did New York and Chicago *combined*.

Alberta architects can no longer complain that economic and political power, and with them quality architecture, reside elsewhere, inaccessible to those in the suburbs of the world. While there are still inadequacies with respect to some building components, western Canada has now established enough of a building products industry to eliminate further excuses for shoddy detailing and maladapted forms. With the ballooning of Alberta's Heritage Fund and the dramatic increases in Canadian ownership of the energy industry, the argument that a branch plant economy breeds branch plant architecture no longer holds.

The problems now confronting Alberta architects are no longer mainly economic, political or technological, but cultural. Does Alberta have an identifiable culture which requires a unique architectural expression? If so, should architects strive for these qualities in all buildings, or just those most closely allied with cultural ambitions, such as galleries or libraries? If regionalism is denied, how will it be possible to get internationalist buildings as innovative and artful as the best of those in the major centres of design?

In the effort either to achieve the best in international architecture, or to forge a meaningful regionalism, architects might take note from prairie artists in other disciplines. Partly through the efforts of New York art critic Clement Greenberg, and the participation of key New York artists at Emma Lake painting workshops in the 1960s, a vibrant school in minimalist painting now lives on in Edmonton and Saskatoon, even while it is dying in New York itself; a cross-continental cha-cha of the Boho Dance described by critic Tom Wolfe in his famous essay, *The Painted Word*.[1]

Prairie writers are even more desirable as models. With the pioneering efforts of Frederick Philip Grove, Wallace Stegner, W.O. Mitchell and Margaret Laurence, followed by the recent work of Rudy Wiebe and Robert Kroetsch, the prairies have developed what now is realized widely to be Canada's most vibrant regional literature. These writers and their younger students are fiercely independent and original in language and topic, and just as fiercely critical of the erosion of a regional culture by the lapping waters of global taste and fashion.

Accomplishing a vibrant regional architecture in Alberta will be much more difficult than launching a local literature. The corporate tendency in architecture and the institutional conservatism of the building industry submerge the efforts of the individual. There is a conceptual inertia that now binds governments, developers, clients, and, of course, architects. Many major buildings are commissioned and designed by committees whose members often converge on a safe common denominator in design and detailing. Perhaps most damaging, the cycle of boom and bust discourages quality architecture at both extremes: architects are either too busy, or not busy enough, to invest the effort needed for the design of an original building.

Of immediate importance, however, is the need to protect those aspects of our built heritage that need it. Alberta now faces a serious problem with respect to the preservation of its Modern architectural resources. A revival of the recent boom would mean that the province's modern architectural heritage may soon share the fate of too much of its sandstone and brick architecture. To cite an ironic example, recent development to house Calgary's oil industry has destroyed many of the buildings associated with its own birth and development. Besides, one does not disassemble the Brown Building and rebuild it in Heritage Park! Future generations may well ask about our wisdom in preserving safely antique Victorian buildings with public funds and policies even while much of the architectural record of the twentieth century bit the dust. We must shake the idea that history, as represented by the shells of buildings, ends in Alberta about 1925.

Virtually every building in this book built before 1960 is threatened. The casualties continue to mount. Nearly 10 percent of all the buildings surveyed since the beginning of research on this book have been demolished. To cite just two examples, the Red Indian Service Station in Calgary was replaced by a low-rise cedar office building; and a sister garage, the Big Chief Service Station, was gutted by fire and replaced by an equally ignoble building. Many more were destroyed in the last years of the boom to make way for parking lots that will endure a generation. Douglas Cardinal's St. Mary's Church in Red Deer has had indiscriminate suburban tract housing creep up literally to its back door. As magnificent a building as Lyle's Calgary Bank of Nova Scotia remained empty for a decade, its demolition stayed by its *ad hoc* conversion to a discothèque.

Through the results of extensive research and writing, and wide recognition of the importance of its recent history, California now protects with heritage site designation more buildings from the post-1925 period than from earlier decades. While California may have more exuberant examples of Modern, Moderne, and International Style architecture than does Alberta, this does not mean that buildings such as the Varscona Theatre and the Barron Building are not worthy of our immediate attention. Effort is now needed if the built cultural legacy of the last few decades is not to join that of the late Victorian and Edwardian eras, too often remembered only in dusty archival photographs or heritage museums.

The extension of the provincial designation programme to Alberta's Modern architectural resources must be preceded by public enlightenment of the historical significance, cultural resonance, even the visual delight of stucco, glass and steel buildings. Maintaining a visual record of half of the twentieth century in Alberta cannot be guaranteed by iron-clad legal designation, but rather by increased appreciation by the public, the development industry, and government, of the sentimental and economic value of these buildings. If their value is demonstrated in both rational and emotional terms, economically viable preservation of post-1925 buildings will follow in many cases.

Critical articles, guidebooks, gallery shows, and a dialogue with the public on what it means to create a culturally integrated architecture are needed if the latest building boom is to result in a unique and lasting architecture. John Lyle proposed what was needed for Canadian architecture fifty years ago:

> I am firmly of the opinion that Canadian architecture will never come into its own unless we can educate public opinion as to what is good or bad architecture, and that criticism is as necessary for the architect's good as for that of the public.[2]

Alberta architecture has gone through a tremendous maturation in the past fifty years. The reestablishment of Victorian historicism or even the humble indigenous stucco tradition that marked the Alberta architecture of the 1920s and 1930s is out of the question. Alberta has become, for architectural good or ill, integrally connected to the global network. Tempered by the atmosphere of constructive criticism that Lyle advocated, we must tame the beast of the boom and use it to shape rich, diverse, and pluralist cities, or else pass on to our children the hulking forms of our failure.

Calgary Civic Building. Courtesy of City of Calgary.

POSTSCRIPT, 1986

Much has happened since the completion in 1981 of the original manuscript of "Modern Architecture in Alberta." The building boom came to an abrupt halt with the recession in 1982, only stirring briefly again in 1985. It now seems certain that the Alberta of the early twenty-first century will be virtually indistinguishable from that of today. Calgary will become a living museum of the architecture of the 1970s in the same way that Winnipeg completely documents the architectural conventions of the decade before World War I. More buildings described in the study were destroyed in the final cycle of the boom, and, bewilderingly, some are threatened even as this is written (the T. Eaton Company store in Edmonton recently received a death sentence in the form of civic approval of the Triple Five Corporation's Eaton Centre, while the Varscona Theatre is similarly threatened). While it is sad that buildings of such architectural importance are lost even in the depths of a recession, there is no chance that Alberta's major urban centres will lose their character as repositories of the architectural expressions of modernism.

The melancholy engendered by the collapse of the building boom is most apparent in Calgary. While some new towers sat empty for months, they have since taken tenants from older towers, such as the Barron Building, bringing the continued existence of buildings of this class into question. Despite their historic merits, these buildings are regarded as second-rate by the iron laws of real estate estimation. There was, however, a marked improvement in the design quality of Calgary office towers in the last few years of the boom. Finishes improved and colours richened, more care was expended on the detailing and proportions of elevations, and the caps of towers came to express more than the existence of mechanical equipment. Sadly, Calgary architecture was just crawling out of the minimalist mirrored box when the boom collapsed.

With the increase in downtown densities, the Plus 15 Bonus System finally became just that, enough of a continuous system that climate protected travel became possible. Calgary has a new Civic Building designed by the Toronto corporate design firm of Webb Zerafa Menkes Housden. This silvered wedge, with Dodd's sandstone 1912 city hall perched nervously nearby, would look comfortable in an oil company research park—perhaps a not unintended or unfortunate choice of imagery for a civic building in Calgary. While Mississauga, Portland, and other centres explore variations of Post-Modernism for civic buildings, Calgary capped its era of greatest expansion with a resolutely modernist structure.

If downtown Calgary speaks of architectural melancholy, for downtown Edmonton the atmosphere has become out and out despair. A combination of events and policies has resulted in the most depressed core of any major Canadian city, taking away this dubious distinction from Winnipeg. While the proliferation of suburban shopping malls is widely blamed for the downtown's demise, other factors must share the blame. Downtown Edmonton ceased to be viable because shoppers, office tenants, government departments, and apartment dwellers chose to locate in more bucolic settings on the fringe of the city, and because there was neither planning nor public policy will to resist this centrifugal force. Like Calgary, however, the quality of downtown office towers vastly improved towards the end of the boom in Edmonton. A case in point is Donald Bittorf's elegantly Late Modernist Principal Plaza. This building caps his distinguished career as one of the province's most consistently good architects, embodying the handsome proportions and lack of accommodation to fashion typical of his works.

In contrast, most shopping malls define all that is sterile and ephemeral in architecture. The West Edmonton Mall, principally designed by Maurice Sunderland, is but the biggest example of this genre which sacrifices

Aerial photograph, West Edmonton Mall, 1986. Courtesy Engineering Division, Transportation Department, City of Edmonton.

exterior detailing for interior glitter. Whether Edmontonians will accept the ersatz urbanism of New Orleans Street or the mock rue Saint Honoré as an ongoing substitute for the downtown they wasted, only time will tell. The process by which Edmonton's core died is underway in every city and town which bets all growth on a mall, which turns former main streets into quaint historic districts, and which trades its own cultural soul for a generic commercialism.

The last cycle of the boom saw an astonishing range and quantity of public buildings constructed throughout the province: every trail crossing and creek fording got its new provincial building, courthouse, or research facility. These buildings were generously funded, they were constructed of the finest materials to withstand the rigours of time, and they were carefully tailored to meet the needs (real or imagined) of the local population. Yet, for the most part, they are overwhelmingly dull, with all but the faintest sparks of art and vigour homogenized by well-meaning committees. There are exceptions, of course, one being the woodsy new courthouse in the village of Breton, that would grace a city of a hundred times the population. Another exception is Edson's smart Provincial Building, designed by Edmonton architect Gene Dub in an amalgam of railway depot and Ukrainian farmhouse styles—an unlikely combination more successful than this description might indicate.

Arthur Erickson's bridge metaphor one liner, the University of Lethbridge, has had its punch line muted by several unsympathetic additions. Drumheller has the Tyrrell Museum of Palaeontology, Devon has the Coal Research Centre, and Athabasca has a university. The St. Albert Civic Centre, designed by Douglas Cardinal, brought a library, theatre, and community classrooms together with town offices and agencies. The interiors are less appealing than some of Cardinal's designs, but the sinuous modelling of the exterior recalls and transforms the landforms of the river valley in which it is sublimely set. The St. Albert Civic Centre may well

Provincial Building, Edson. Courtesy of Dub Architects Ltd.

be Cardinal's last work in his native province. Like an entire generation of architects, Cardinal has left the province, there being little use for architects when boom turns to bust. His Museum of Civilization rises above the Ottawa River and Cardinal's new home, a prairie building finding its roots in a strange eastern setting. One cannot help but think of A.M. Jeffers, designer of the Edmonton Legislative Building, and his sad journey to Prince Rupert, then to California, when an over-built province had no buildings for any but the best-connected of designers after World War I.

Post-Modernism has progressed from a fringe movement to the style of choice for buildings constructed during the recession, the style emerging as a visual analogue to the return to the traditional values (often not traditional at all) trumpeted by the neo-conservatives. Post-Modern design work in the province is uneven, including both the best and the worst of buildings in the past half decade. Among the best are designs by the Calgary firm, the Sturgess Partnership, which have progressed steadily from house additions to multi-family housing, from mansions for oil barons and now to public buildings. The hallmarks of this firm are a lively,

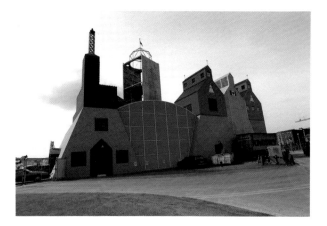

Alberta Pavilion at Expo 86. Courtesy Public Affairs Bureau, Government of Alberta.

playful approach to both symbolism and colour balanced by careful attention to programming and management. Their greatest acclaim came in response to their design for the Alberta Pavilion at Expo 86, a collage of visual references to the province's industries and building types, translated into a trendy argot borrowed from Graves, Rossi, and other architects.

In Edmonton, Post-Modernism has received a boost from the Public School Board, which has invested in quality design together with durable materials and finishes. The most recent school buildings in Edmonton have included some unabashedly Post-Modern creations of considerable symbolic power and urban grace. Richard L. Wilkin's Tapaskan School in Millwoods is based on a flexible and designed-for-growth pedestrian spine, with the various programme elements given individual architectural expression. The result can be likened to a nineteenth-century prairie town centre, complete with town hall, church and commercial buildings, and it provides a welcome landmark and playful visual relief in the dreary depths of Edmonton's Millwoods district. Barry Johns's Julia Kiniski Elementary School, also in Millwoods, does not have the flexibility of Wilkin's plan, but its simpler civic symbolism may work even better. The bell tower and roof modelling give this tiny school a surprisingly monumental quality, and the interior is filled with fun and quirky detailing.

A recent trip to Austin, Texas, has tempered my criticism of the shoddiness and the austerity of the modernist legacy in downtown Edmonton and Calgary. Austin's boom started in 1982, at about the time that Alberta's ground to a halt. The stylistic latitude afforded by Post-Modernism and its derivatives can create results just as dreary as any by Modernism's students, and Austin's new downtown buildings demonstrate that poorly designed Post-Modernism is no better, probably worse, than poorly designed Modernism. Seeing such buildings renewed my belief that the most important issues facing contemporary architects have to do not with style, but with the integration of a building into its social, historical, environmental, and cultural setting; in short, regionalism.

What are we to make of the modernist legacy in Alberta buildings? For those rare buildings, like Hemingway's Stanley Engineering Building, where texture, colour, and proportion fuse with programme and material to make a stunning building, the best of high art modernism is clearly in evidence. But the buildings from the final cycle of Modern architecture in Alberta, 1975-85, simply do not compare to those designed in the early 1970s by the generation of Atkins, Long, Cardinal, Hemingway, Bittorf, and others. By the early 1980s, Modernism had severed all links with the social vision and formal innovation of its founders—it had grown fat and stupid, a parody of the spirit of innovation which was its spark, and it deserved to die. Alberta now faces a problem of learning to live semi-permanently with its modernist legacy, a bewildering dilemma because there was no constant in its architecture but change, no principle but demolition and renewal, no ideology but the booster's optimism. Marshall Berman's brilliant book on modernism, *All That Is Solid Melts Into Air*,[1] takes its poetic title from a line in Marx about the constancy of change in the modern condition. For Alberta architecture, all that is solid has melted into air. And now it is going to rain for a while.

Trevor Boddy
Pigeon Lake and Vancouver
September 1986

Julia Kiniski Elementary School. Courtesy Barry Johns Architect Ltd. Photograph by Jim Dow.

Stucco Vernacular building at Thorsby.

APPENDIX
A SAMPLER OF MODERN STYLES

Stucco Vernacular

Stucco Vernacular building in Thorsby, 1930-50

Features:

- humble white stucco buildings that both inspired and later themselves drew inspiration from Modern architecture in its high style variants
- rounded corners, overhanging parapets
- stucco is normally applied over a wire mesh on a plywood or board surface
- a variety of finishing surfaces can be made including rustication, quoining, corbelling, broken glass wash, coloured mortar, or whitewash

Art Deco details from the York Hotel, Calgary, 1928.

Art Deco

The Examiner Building, Calgary, 1931

Art Deco details from the York Hotel, Calgary, 1928

Features:

- named for the 1925 Paris Exposition Internationale des Arts Décoratifs et Industriels Modernes
- the most ornamental and transitional of the modern styles
- extensive use of zigzag, chevron, sunburst, wave, spiral, and stylized plant ornamental motifs, usually in low sculpted relief
- symmetry and balance, often with a central tower
- stepped back ''wedding cake'' building massing

The Examiner Building, Calgary, 1931. H. Pollard Collection, Provincial Archives of Alberta.

Moderne

Crossroads of the World, Los Angeles by R. Derrah, 1936

The Dreamland Theatre, Edmonton, by Rule Wynn and Rule, demolished 1980.

Features:

- white stucco boxes with streamlined rounded corners or parapets
- horizontal emphasis obtained through banded surfaces or windows often painted in contrasting colours
- use of glass, brick or portal windows
- use of wings, fins or protruding bands
- allusions to forms of transport or other machinery

The Dreamland Theatre, Edmonton, by Rule Wynn and Rule. Glenbow-Alberta Institute, Calgary.

Crossroads of the World, Los Angeles, by R. Derrah, 1936.

The Bauhaus School, Dessau, Germany, by Walter Gropius, 1925-26. Photograph courtesy of The Museum of Modern Art, New York.

Exterior, Housing Union Building, a student residence at the University of Alberta, by Wilkin-Diamond-Myers, 1974. Photograph by Trig Singer.

International Style: Gropius/Bauhaus

The Bauhaus School of Design, Walter Gropius, 1925

Housing Union Building student residence, University of Alberta, by Wilkin-Diamond-Myers, 1974

Features:

- total elimination of ornament; planar, often white surfaces
- off-centre composition, extremely rational and functional space planning
- continuous horizontal, or ribbon, windows
- emphasis on Total Design; singular organizing design principles from hardware and furniture, through city planning, with a strong emphasis on the Platonic solid geometric forms

The Stanley Engineering Building, Edmonton, by Peter
Hemingway, 1970.

The Seagram Tower, New York, by Mies van der Rohe and
Philip Johnson.

International Style: Miesian

The Seagram Tower, New York, by Mies van der Rohe and
Philip Johnson

The Stanley Engineering Building, Edmonton, by Peter
Hemingway, 1970

Features:

- rigidly and exclusively rectilinear form, with strong
  emphasis on proportion and balance
- meticulous attention to details, especially window
  mullions, doors
- a richness of material surface counters, a stripped-down
  design philosophy
- often uses steel I-beams to "express the structure," but
  these functional-looking beams may be present only for
  decorative, shadow casting purposes
- the glass box, redone at any scale, anywhere, for any use

International Style: Corbusian

The Villa Savoye by Le Corbusier, 1929-30

Interior

The Cross House in Calgary's Mount Royal Area, circa 1942

Features:

- planar white, often stucco, wall surfaces broken by horizontal banded windows
- blocky, formal composition
- limited use of circular building elements to contrast with overall rectilinearity
- building often lifted off the ground by means of ''pilotis'' or free standing posts

The Villa Savoye, Poissy-sur-Seine, by Le Corbusier, 1929-30. Photograph courtesy of The Museum of Modern Art, New York.

The Villa Savoye, showing the entrance-hall in construction. Photograph courtesy of The Museum of Modern Art, New York.

The Cross House, in Calgary's Mount Royal area, circa 1942.

The Cross House, showing its horizontal banded windows.

The National Theatre, Southbank, London, by Denys Lasdun, 1976.

The Brutalist architecture of the National Theatre, Southbank, London.

The Edmonton Art Gallery, by Bittorf-Wensley Architects, 1969.

Brutalist

The National Theatre, Southbank, London, 1976, by Denys Lasdun

The Edmonton Art Gallery by Don Bittorf, 1969

Features:

- a style largely inspired by the later works of Le Corbusier
- rough texture, stippled, bare aggregate or board-forming concrete is the most common material, often highlighted by steel or glass
- different concrete finishes or colours used adjacently
- formal, heavy composition

The Yale University Art Centre, by Louis Kahn, 1970.

The Stony Tribal Administration Centre, Morley, by Gordon Atkins, 1979. Courtesy Atkins Architects.

Late Modern

The Yale University Art Centre by Louis Kahn, 1970

The Stony Tribal Administration Centre, Morley, by Gordon Atkins, 1979

Features:

- the work of Alvar Aalto of Finland and Louis Kahn of the United States established a warmer, more humanistic strain of Modern architecture around the middle of the twentieth century
- warmer colours and richer palette of cladding materials than high Modern architecture; strong emphasis on brick and wood
- more concern with contextual issues, adapting to the urban fabric

Interior, Stony Tribal Administration Centre, Morley. Courtesy Atkins Architects.

Cafe Calabash, Calgary, by Daniel Jenkins, 1980.
Photograph by Morten Bot.

Post-Modern

The Benjamin Franklin Memorial Museum, by Venturi and Rauch, 1963

Cafe Calabash, Calgary, by Daniel Jenkins, 1980

Features:

- more defined for what it is not—functional, rational, modern—than for what it is
- reintroduction of decoration, bright colour and graphics
- historical reference, reintroduction of the classical order
- design choices opt for the complex and the contradictory, the ugly and the ordinary
- issues of contextualism vis-à-vis the city and built tradition become important

The Benjamin Franklin Memorial Museum, Philadelphia, by Venturi and Rauch, 1963.

NOTES

Introduction

1 Stephen Spender, "The Modern as Vision of the Whole," in *The Idea of the Modern in Literature and the Arts*, ed. Irving Howe (New York: Horizon Press, 1967), 51.

2 Colin Rowe and Fred Koetter, *Collage City* (Cambridge, Mass.: MIT Press, 1978), 4.

3 Adolf Loos, "Ornament and Crime," in *Sämtliche Schriften*, vol. 1, ed. Franz Gluck (Vienna: Herold, 1962), 276-87. The essay, first published in 1908, was reprinted throughout Europe and was known to have influenced Mies van der Rohe, Le Corbusier, and others.

4 Irving Howe, *The Idea of the Modern in Literature and the Arts* (New York: Horizon Press, 1967), 18.

5 For an example, see Le Corbusier's Villa Savoye in the Appendix, "A Sampler of Modern Styles."

1. The Decline of Historicism

1 The British label buildings of this period Edwardian architecture, while the Americans call them Late Victorian. Predictably, Canadians use both terms.

2 Edmund Herbert Dale, "The Role of Successive Town and City Councils in the Evolution of Edmonton, Alberta, 1892 to 1966" (Ph.D. dissertation, University of Alberta, 1969), 168.

3 See Diana L. Bodnar, "The Prairie Legislative Buildings of Canada" (Master's thesis, University of British Columbia, 1979), 25-26.

4 The records of the Alberta Association of Architects (AAA) are housed in the Canadian Architectural Archives at the University of Calgary. Membership lists, which included addresses, were also published in the Royal Architectural Institute of Canada (RAIC) *Journal* throughout the 1920s. A complete set of these publications is located in the Rutherford Library, University of Alberta, Edmonton.

5 For an interesting exploration of this regional vernacular, see *Edmonton Entrances*, the catalogue of an exhibition organized by The Edmonton Art Gallery, 3 November to 10 December 1975.

6 John Lehr, *Ukrainian Vernacular Architecture in Alberta*, Alberta Culture, Historic Sites Service Occasional Paper no. 1 (Edmonton, Alberta, 1976).

7 Mary-Etta MacPherson, "The Canadian House of Today," *Canadian Homes and Gardens* (June 1929) 17-20, 51, 52.

8 Ibid., 17.

9 Report to the Calgary Performing Arts Centre Advisory Group by Theatre Projects Consultants of London, 1979. A more recent example of the architectural conservatism of some governments is the construction in the 1970s of the fifties-style Brutalist National Theatre in London by Denys Lasdun. To be fair, for both the British and Calgary examples, the source of their conservatism may be their size—both are relatively large projects. With occasional exceptions, most architectural innovations are made in small projects.

10 Members of the Al Raschid Mosque, the Edmonton Historical Society, and officials of Alberta Culture, Historic Sites Service, have corresponded with other long-established Islamic communities throughout North America. This correspondence revealed that while there are older mosques, they are in converted buildings.

11 Ivan Danylo Harach, "A Report on St. Josaphat's Ukrainian Catholic Cathedral," Department of Academic Studies, Northern Alberta Institute of Technology (NAIT), Edmonton, Alberta, 25 April 1969. This study and others are available at the City of Edmonton Archives. The

133

student projects done by NAIT and University of Calgary students are among the earliest pieces of architectural history research conducted in Alberta.

12 The oldest remaining Mormon temple in Alberta is a wood frame structure built in the 1890s at Raymond. It is an indication of the religious and ethnic tolerance that characterized much of Alberta society that this church, which is still owned by the Church of Jesus Christ of Latter-Day Saints, is now used as a Buddhist temple by the large local Japanese and Tibetan population.

13 Laurel B. Andrew, *The Early Temples of the Mormons: The Architecture of the Millennial Kingdom in the American West* (Albany, New York: State University of New York Press, 1977), 24.

14 It was perhaps too long and low. All three persons interviewed who had been inside the building remarked on its dark and narrow qualities, which resulted in a feeling of claustrophobia.

15 Address by John M. Lyle to the RAIC, 22 February 1929, at the Art Gallery of Ontario, Toronto. Published in the RAIC *Journal* (April 1929): 135.

16 Ibid.

17 *The Silent Partner* (Edmonton, Alberta: Alberta Government Telephones, December 1930), 11.

18 Address by John M. Lyle to the RAIC, 22 February 1929, at the Art Gallery of Ontario, Toronto. Published in the RAIC *Journal* (April 1929): 136.

19 See John M. Lyle, "Recent Architecture of the Bank of Nova Scotia," *The Canadian Banker* 44 (January 1937): 150-57.

20 Thomas S. Kuhn, *The Structure of Scientific Revolutions*, 2nd. ed. (Chicago: University of Chicago Press, 1970), see especially Chapters 5 through 7.

2. Sources of Modernism

1 Although castigated by present-day critics as an apologist for the movement, Nikolaus Pevsner is particularly lucid in teasing out the many competing threads that combined to form the Modern Movement in architecture. Pevsner's *The Sources of Modern Architecture and Design* (New York: Praeger, 1968), and his *Pioneers of the Modern Movement from William Morris to Walter Gropius*, rev. ed. (Harmondsworth: Penguin Books, Ltd., 1960), give excellent overviews of the many elements of European art and design that came together to form that amorphous design ideology we now call the Modern Movement.

2 See Herbert Bayer, Walter Gropius, and Ise Gropius (eds.), *The Bauhaus: 1919-1928* (New York: The Museum of Modern Art, 1938), 14.

3 Ayn Rand's *The Fountainhead* (Indianapolis: Bobbs-Merrill, 1968) is the best-known depiction in fiction of this shallow and dangerous caricature. She modelled her protagonist loosely on Frank Lloyd Wright, and this towering best-seller led a whole generation of incipient Objectivists to architecture school.

4 Neutra visited Alberta several times in the 1950s as a guest of the important "Banff Session" conference; earlier visits to Vancouver helped to promote the establishment of the University of British Columbia School of Architecture.

5 Le Corbusier [Charles-Edouard Jeanneret-Gris], *Vers Une Architecture* (Paris: Les Editions G. Cres et Cie., 1923). English translation *Towards a New Architecture* (London: John Rodker, 1931).

6 This building was incorrectly placed by Melvin Charney and others at the Lakehead. Pollard's negative of the photograph used by Le Corbusier is now in the Provincial Archives of Alberta in Edmonton.

7 Henry-Russell Hitchcock, Jr., *Modern Architecture: Romanticism and Reintegration* (New York: Payson and Clarke, Ltd., 1929).

8 Henry-Russell Hitchcock, Jr., and Philip Johnson, *The International Style: Architecture Since 1922* (New York: W.W. Norton, 1932).

9 The characteristics of these and other twentieth-century architectural styles are described in the Appendix, "A Sampler of Modern Styles."

10 The first entries in Henderson's Directories for service stations on the two sites appeared in these years. Parts of

the fin-like streamlined sign towers may have been additions from the thirties.

11 *The Silent Partner* (Edmonton: Alberta Government Telephones, July 1929), 8.

12 *The Silent Partner* (Edmonton: Alberta Government Telephones, October 1930), 11.

13 John Ruskin, *The Seven Lamps of Architecture* (New York: The Noonday Press, 1974).

14 Augustus Welby Northmore Pugin, *The True Principles of Pointed or Christian Architecture: Set Forth in Two Lectures Delivered at St. Marie's, Oscott* (London: J. Weale, 1841).

15 Eugène Emmanuel Viollet-le-Duc, *Discourses on Architecture*, trans. Benjamin Bucknall (New York: Grove Press, Inc., 1959).

16 Rietveld and Mondrian were Dutch painters who did much to establish the rectilinear geometric aesthetic which has inspired the bulk of Modern Movement architecture. The movement is sometimes called Elementarism, as it dealt with the basics of perception and supposedly primary colours, in lines, the grid. Charles Rennie MacIntosh was a long-neglected Glasgow architect who anticipated many Modern Movement aesthetic and technical developments. The detailing of the light fixtures of the library of his Glasgow School of Art employs a sparse decorative grid not unlike that used by Rule on his windows.

17 George Lord, a partner in Rule's successor firm, now Forbes, Lord, Feldberg, Schmidt, Croll, interview with author, Edmonton, Alberta, April 1980.

18 W.A.R. Kerr to C.S. Burgess, 10 April 1939, Cecil Burgess Papers, University of Alberta Archives.

19 With current traffic loads one no longer enjoys traffic circles, but for many years they were an urbane way of circulating through Alberta's capital city.

20 A definition and examples of Moderne, along with other architectural styles, are to be found in the Appendix, "A Sampler of Modern Styles."

21 *The Edmonton Bulletin*, 6 July 1940.

22 See the Appendix, "A Sampler of Modern Styles," for additional examples of some of these figures.

23 The architectural drawings for the Varscona Theatre, along with those for all buildings of both the Calgary and Edmonton offices of Rule Wynn and Rule, are in the collection of the Canadian Architectural Archives, University of Calgary.

3. Modern Architecture in Alberta

1 According to Mr. Barron's son, Robert H. Barron, this was the largest mortgage that Great West Life Assurance Company granted on a development up to that time. The twenty-year mortgage carried what then was regarded by some as exhorbitant interest of 4½ percent. There was also a second mortgage of $250,000 granted by J. Arthur Rank's Odeon Theatres.

2 This style unfortunately seems to be identified with large, oppressive institutions. It has been referred to as Mussolini Modern or J. Edgar Hoover Neo-Classical.

3 The Plus 15 Bonus System was conceived in the 1960s as a way of making Calgary's downtown area more attractive to pedestrians. A system of covered walkways connecting downtown towers fifteen feet above ground level separated the pedestrian from vehicular traffic, sheltered him from the weather, and simplified movement between buildings. Developers receive bonuses for including the walkways and the adjacent open and amenity spaces in their complexes.

4 University of Alberta urban geographer Denis Johnson and his colleague F.W. Boal published a study of the urban forces at work on the Macleod Trail that was among the first to pay serious academic attention to this new urban form. See "The Functions of Retail and Service Establishments on Commercial Ribbons," in *Internal Structure of the City: Readings on Urban Form, Growth and Policy*, ed. L.S. Bourne (New York: Oxford University Press, 1971), 368-79.

5 Lyle's quote appears in the RAIC *Journal* 9 (March 1932): 70. Alberta schools included architecture in their curricula and newspapers featured architectural criticism before World War I. Today, both are virtually non-existent.

6 Edmonton-born McLuhan's best study of this type is *The Mechanical Bride: Folklore of Industrial Man* (New York: Vanguard Press, 1951).

7 Robert Venturi, Denise Scott Brown and Steven Izenour, *Learning from Las Vegas: The Forgotten Symbolism of Architectural Form*, 2nd. ed. (Cambridge, Mass.: MIT Press, 1977). See especially Part Two.

8 See the Appendix, "A Sampler of Modern Styles."

9 McLuhan based many of his theories regarding culture and communication on the notions of Canadian historian H.A. Innis. Innis looked at frontier Canada and saw how modes of communication shaped the entire form of early Canadian society.

10 This is not to belittle these firms. They are among the first architectural practices to utilize behavioural information in the design process to make these buildings more efficient and profitable. While many architects talk of the possible input of the social sciences into architectural design, the orange lighting and seat design of, for example, a Denny's restaurant, are the built result of behavioural research, the colours to encourage extra ordering, the seats to create discomfort after twenty-two minutes.

11 The Housing Union Building (HUB), a student residence at the University of Alberta, designed by Jack Diamond and Barton Myers in association with Richard L. Wilkin, and the University of Lethbridge by Arthur Erickson, are two dreams of megastructure that actually saw realization in Alberta during the reign of Modern architecture.

4. Towards an Alberta Architecture

1 Béton brut, literally crude concrete or concrete in the raw, is concrete left in its natural state after formwork has been removed. It was much favoured by Le Corbusier in later projects, such as the Dominican Friary at La Tourette and the Church at Ronchamp. It achieved great popularity in Canada in the late 1960s.

2 Philip Johnson, interview with the author, New York, 1980.

3 George Melnyk (ed.), *Of the Spirit: Writings by Douglas Cardinal* (Edmonton: NeWest Press, 1977), 36.

Conclusion

1 Tom Wolfe has recently turned the wit and the arguments found in *The Painted Word* (New York: Farrar Straus and Giroux, 1975) to the story of the capitulation of American architecture to European-style modernism in *From Bauhaus to Our House* (New York: Farrar Straus and Giroux, 1981).

2 Address by John M. Lyle to the RAIC, 22 February 1929, at the Art Gallery of Ontario, Toronto. Published in the RAIC *Journal* (April 1929): 136.

Postscript

1 Marshall Berman, *All That Is Solid Melts Into Air: The Experience of Modernity* (New York: Simon and Schuster, 1982).

BIBLIOGRAPHY

Allen, Richard, ed. *A Region of the Mind: Interpreting the Western Canadian Plains*. Regina: Canadian Plains Research Center, University of Regina, 1973.

Andrew, Laurel B. *The Early Temples of the Mormons: The Architecture of the Millennial Kingdom in the American West*. Albany: State University of New York Press, 1977.

Andrews, Wayne. *Architecture, Ambition and Americans*. New York: Harper and Brothers, 1947.

Artibise, Alan F.J. "Urban Development in Western Canada." Paper presented at the 1978 Western Canadian Studies Conference, University of Calgary, February 1978.

Artscanada. Issue Number 218/219, February/March 1978.

Banham, Reyner. *Theory and Design in the First Machine Age*. London: Architectural Press, 1960.

Bayer, Herbert, Walter Gropius, and Ise Gropius, eds. *The Bauhaus: 1919-1928*. New York: Museum of Modern Art, 1938.

Bebout, Richard, ed. *The Open Gate: Toronto Union Station*. Toronto: Peter Martin Associates, 1972.

Berman, Marshall. *All That Is Solid Melts Into Air: The Experience of Modernity*. New York: Simon and Schuster, 1982.

Bodnar, Diana L. "The Prairie Legislative Buildings of Canada." Master's thesis, University of British Columbia, 1979.

Brambilla, Roberto, and Gianni Longo. *For Pedestrians Only: Planning, Design, and Management of Traffic-Free Zones*. New York: Billboard Publications, Inc., 1977.

Brooks, H. Allen. *The Prairie School: Frank Lloyd Wright and his Midwest Contemporaries*. Toronto: University of Toronto Press, 1972.

The Canadian Architect. Vol. 15, No. 9, September 1970; Vol. 16, No. 4, April 1971; Vol. 22, No. 9, September 1977; Vol. 23, No. 1, January 1978; Vol. 23, No. 3, March 1978.

The Canadian Architect Yearbook, 1970. Don Mills, Ontario: Southam Business Publications.

Colgate, William G. *Canadian Art: Its Origin and Development*. Toronto: The Ryerson Press, 1943.

Dale, Edmund H. "The Role of Successive Town and City Councils in the Evolution of Edmonton, Alberta, 1892 to 1966." Ph.D. dissertation, University of Alberta, 1969.

The Edmonton Bulletin. "Mayor Takes Part in Official Opening South Side Theatre," 6 July 1940. "The Varscona Theatre," 9 May 1940. "New Movie Palace Built for Comfort: Seats 780 Patrons," 24 October 1940.

Edmonton Entrances. Catalogue of an exhibition organized by The Edmonton Art Gallery, 3 November to 10 December 1975.

Fleming, John, Hugh Honour, and Nikolaus Pevsner, eds. *The Penguin Dictionary of Architecture*. Harmondsworth: Penguin Books, 1966.

Francaviglia, Richard V. *The Mormon Landscape: Existence, Creation, and Perception of a Unique Image in the American West*. New York: AMS Press, 1978.

Frankl, Paul. *Principles of Architectural History: The Four Phases of Architectural Style, 1420-1900*. Translated and edited by James F. O'Gormon. Cambridge, Mass.: MIT Press, 1968.

Gebhard, David, and Harriette Von Breton. *L.A. in the Thirties: 1931-1941*. Layton, Utah: Peregrine Smith Inc., 1975.

Giedion, Siegfried. *Space, Time and Architecture: The Growth of a New Tradition*. Cambridge, Mass.: Harvard University Press, 1949.

Gowans, Alan. *Building Canada: An Architectural History of Canadian Life*. Toronto: Oxford University Press, 1966.

Gray, James H. *Boomtime: Peopling the Canadian Prairies*. Saskatoon: Western Producer Prairie Books, 1979.

Gropius, Walter. *The New Architecture and the Bauhaus*. Translated by P. Morton Shand. Cambridge, Mass.: MIT Press, 1965.

Harach, Ivan Danylo. "A Report on St. Josaphat's Ukrainian Catholic Cathedral," Department of Academic Studies, NAIT, Edmonton, Alberta, April 25, 1969, unpublished.

Hitchcock, Henry-Russell, Jr. *Modern Architecture: Romanticism and Reintegration*. New York: Payson and Clarke, Ltd., 1929.

Hitchcock, Henry-Russell, Jr., and Philip Johnson. *The International Style: Architecture Since 1922*. New York: W.W. Norton & Company, Inc., 1966.

Howe, Irving. *The Idea of the Modern in Literature and the Arts*. New York: Horizon Press, 1967.

Jackson, Anthony. *The Democratization of Canadian Architecture*. Halifax: Tech-Press, 1978.

_____ . *The Future of Canadian Architecture*. Halifax: Tech-Press, 1979.

Jencks, Charles. *Modern Movements in Architecture*. Garden City, New York: Anchor Press, 1973.

Johnson, Philip C. *Mies van der Rohe*. 3rd ed., rev., New York: Museum of Modern Art, 1978.

Johnson, Denis, and F.W. Boal. "The Functions of Retail and Service Establishments on Commercial Ribbons." In *Internal Structure of the City: Readings on Urban Form, Growth and Policy*, edited by L.S. Bourne. New York: Oxford University Press, 1971.

Jordy, William H. *American Buildings and their Architects*. New York: Anchor Press, 1976.

Kuhn, Thomas S. *The Structure of Scientific Revolutions*. 2nd ed., Chicago: University of Chicago Press, 1970.

Le Corbusier [Jeanneret-Gris, Charles-Edouard]. *New World of Space*. New York: Reynal & Hitchcock, 1948.

_____ . *Vers Une Architecture*. Paris: Les Editions G. Cres et Cie., 1923. [English translation *Towards a New Architecture*. London: John Rodker Publisher, 1931.]

Lehr, John. *Ukrainian Vernacular Architecture in Alberta*. Historic Sites Service Occasional Paper no. 1. Edmonton: Alberta Culture, 1976.

Loos, Adolf. "Ornament and Crime." In *Sämtliche Schriften*, vol. 2, edited by Franz Gluck. Vienna: Herold, 1962.

Lyle, John M. "Recent Architecture of the Bank of Nova Scotia." *The Canadian Banker* 44, no. 2 (January 1937): 150-57.

MacPherson, Mary-Etta. "The Canadian House of Today." *Canadian Homes and Gardens*. June 1929.

Margolies, John. "Pump and Circumstance." *New York Sunday News*, 2 January 1977.

McLuhan, Marshall. *The Mechanical Bride: Folklore of Industrial Man*. New York: Vanguard Press, 1951.

Melnyk, George, ed. *Of the Spirit: Writings by Douglas Cardinal*. Edmonton: NeWest Press, 1977.

Pevsner, Nikolaus. *Pioneers of the Modern Movement from William Morris to Walter Gropius*. Rev. ed., Harmondsworth: Penguin Books, 1960.

_____ . *The Sources of Modern Architecture and Design*. New York: Praeger, 1968.

Poppliers, John, S. Allen Chambers, Jr., and Nancy B. Swartz. *What Style Is It?: A Guide to American Architecture*. Washington, D.C.: The Preservation Press, 1977.

Process: Architecture No. 5. A Perspective of Modern Canadian Architecture. Tokyo: Process Architecture Publishing Co., Ltd., 1978.

Pugin, Augustus Welby Northmore. *The True Principles of Pointed or Christian Architecture*. London: J. Weale, 1841.

Rand, Ayn. *The Fountainhead*. Indianapolis: Bobbs-Merrill, 1968.

Rapoport, Amos. *House Form and Culture*. Englewood Cliffs, N.J.: Prentice-Hall Inc., 1969.

Ritchie, T. *Canada Builds, 1867-1967*. Toronto: University of Toronto Press for the National Research Council of Canada, 1967.

Rowe, Colin, and Fred Koetter. *Collage City*. Cambridge, Mass.: MIT Press, 1978.

Royal Architectural Institute of Canada *Journal*, April 1929.

Ruskin, John. *The Seven Lamps of Architecture*. New York: The Noonday Press, 1974.

Sharp, Dennis, *Sources of Modern Architecture: A Bibliography*. Architectural Association Paper (London) Number 2. New York: George Wittenborn, 1967.

The Silent Partner. "New Exchange Building at Drumheller," July 1929. "New Main Exchange Building for Calgary," October 1929. "Calgary's New Telephone Building Designed to Give the Utmost in Service," October 1930. "New Heights in Calgary's Sky Line," December 1930. Calgary: Alberta Government Telephones.

Spender, Stephen. "The Modern as Vision of the Whole." In *The Idea of the Modern in Literature and the Arts*, edited by Irving Howe. New York: Horizon Press, 1967.

Theatre Projects Consultants of London, Report to the Calgary Performing Arts Centre Advisory Group, 1979.

Venturi, Robert. *Complexity and Contradiction in Architecture*. 2nd. ed., New York: Museum of Modern Art, 1977.

_____ , Denise Scott Brown, and Steven Izenour. *Learning from Las Vegas: The Forgotten Symbolism of Architectural Form*. 2nd. ed., Cambridge, Mass.: MIT Press, 1972.

Viollet-le-Duc, Eugène Emmanuel. *Discourses on Architecture*. New York: Grove Press, Inc., 1959.

Weightman, John. *The Concept of the Avant-Garde: Explorations in Modernism*. London: Alcove Press, 1973.

Wolfe, Tom. *From Bauhaus to Our House*. New York: Farrar Straus and Giroux, 1981.

Zolkewski, Henry A. "A Report on the Al Raschid Mosque." Unpublished, 1969. Department of Academic Studies, NAIT, Edmonton, Alberta, April 25, 1969.

INDEX